HOME INVASION

PROTECTING YOUR FAMILY IN A CULTURE THAT'S GONE STARK RAVING MAD

REBECCA HAGELIN

NELSON CURRENT

A Subsidiary of Thomas Nelson, Inc.

www.nelsoncurrent.com

Published in Nashville, Tennessee, by Nelson Current, a division of a wholly-owned subsidiary (Nelson Communications, Inc.) of Thomas Nelson, Inc.

Nelson Current books may be purchased in bulk for educational, business, fundraising, or sales promotional use. For information, please email SpecialMarkets@ThomasNelson.com.

Library of Congress Cataloging-in-Publication Data

Hagelin, Rebecca.
    Home invasion : protecting your family in a culture that's gone stark raving mad / Rebecca Hagelin.
        p. cm.
    ISBN 1-59555-007-0
    1. Parenting. 2. Parenting—Religious aspects. I. Title.
    HQ755.8.H3315 2005
    306.85'0973—dc22

                                                                                    2004028981

Printed in the United States of America

05 06 07 08 09 QW 7 6 5 4

CONTENTS

Dedicated to my husband, Andy,
and our children, Drew, Nick, and Kristin.

The goal of my heart is to
be the wife and mother God intended for me to be.

———

Home Invasion is also dedicated to all the good parents, grandparents, and youth leaders who just want to do right by today's kids. I don't pretend to have all the answers—many of you have great wisdom and sweet victories that can inspire others. To share your stories, solutions, successes (and even failures) for possible inclusion in a future book, please e-mail them to me at HomeInvasion@ThomasNelson.com.

(NOTE: Identities and e-mail addresses will be kept confidential. Only first names will be used for publication.)

ACKNOWLEDGMENTS

While seated in the stylist's chair at the salon waiting to have my hair trimmed, the tears suddenly came. My only warning was the intense burning I felt in the back of my eyes—I knew I would have to fight extra hard to keep the tears at bay.

Alas, my best efforts proved futile as first one, then two tiny droplets slipped from my eyes and trickled down my cheeks. Mercifully, I got them under control just as I was beginning to fear being overtaken by a gushing flood.

That day marked the end of a difficult, emotional year. One year ago to that bright, spring morning, my father's body was put beneath the damp earth. Within the span of twelve brief weeks, I numbly found myself in that same graveyard as my precious mother's cancer-ridden shell was placed in the ground beside her beloved husband of forty-five years.

As fate would have it, at the precise moment I began to conquer the tears my eleven-year-old daughter, Kristin, appeared squarely in front of me to show off her new haircut. Despite my best smile and most enthusiastic expression, this sensitive, wonderful creature immediately spotted the slight glimmer on my face. She silently reached out with her delicate finger and softly touched a single tear on my left cheek.

Her lovely hazel eyes were filled with compassion and concern as I whispered, "I was just thinking about Papa and Mamma Doc." She nodded, pressed her lips together, and patted my hand. In an instant, my sadness was replaced with the warm glow of knowing that although both of my parents are gone, their legacy of love and compassion are alive and well in my own children.

Losing both parents in the same year was devastating. But in my mourning, God, in His wonderful, mystical way, provided me with an amazing opportunity to help preserve the rich heritage my parents spent their lives protecting. Just as their spirits were going to their eternal destiny, my time here on Earth was being redirected by a strong, unseen hand to what I believe was the privilege of a lifetime: I was offered a position at The Heritage Foundation.

"Without a heritage, every generation starts over." I've spent a lot of time reflecting on the truth of that statement from a Heritage brochure. My childhood was marked by an invaluable treasure. My parents believed that America is a land created by men and women who value virtuous freedom as the ultimate prize, and who know that it is capable of bringing untold joy and satisfaction to those who cherish it.

And Mom and Dad made sure my siblings and I understood this heritage, too. They were involved in struggles to hold back unnecessary government intrusion into the lives of ordinary Americans; lived by principles of faith; created a home environment of love, joy, and independence; and gave of their time, their hearts, and their pockets to better the lives of others—all the while holding a creeping culture at bay.

My father worked diligently as a learned and respected pediatrician for over forty years. He was a man of intelligence, generosity, and undying compassion for the suffering. Dad always saw people as human creatures with needs. You could be certain that if Papa Doc was talking with you, he was also looking you over to see if there might be some sign of a malady. He couldn't help it . . . he was a physician inside and out, first and foremost.

His inherent sense of civic responsibility made it second nature for him to give up the one afternoon he had off each week to volunteer at a kidney clinic for impoverished children. Love of faith and freedom caused our nation's founding fathers to create a land of equal opportunity for all Americans. This same spirit caused my father to spend his life bettering the lives of everyone he could, using the talents that were uniquely his. Both Mom and Dad understood the necessity of preserving America's civil society, and they worked hard to insure it for the next generation.

Mom and Dad would be so very proud to know where I am today. Imagine, their daughter, a member of The Heritage Foundation team. As I work daily with my colleagues at The Heritage Foundation to "build an America where freedom, opportunity, prosperity, and civil society flourish," I am constantly aware that through our work we are making a difference in the lives of our own children and future generations.

It's an honor to give special thanks to my colleagues at Heritage whose hard work produced much of the research I reference in this book. Of particular note is the work of the many experts in our Domestic Policy Department and our Richard and

Helen De Vos Center on Religion and Civil Society, especially the policy analysts Jennifer Marshall and Melissa Pardue who helped me compile the relevant studies for this book. Many thanks also go to Paul Gallagher, whose incredible organizational skills, deep understanding and support of my mission, and skillful eye for editing helped bring this work together. And thanks to my assistant, Tori Ueltschi, who started working with me during the mayhem days of the project, but took the craziness of my schedule in stride—thanks for your professionalism, attention to detail, and calm demeanor. And to my colleague, Becky Norton Dunlop for having been a great supporter of my work and a true friend in the cultural battle for over thirteen years—my undying gratitude. Your friendship is a treasure.

And thank you to Ed Feulner and Phil Truluck for the faith you have placed in me, and for the opportunity of a lifetime to serve The Heritage Foundation and this America that I love so deeply.

I also owe a huge debt of gratitude to Joseph Farah, David Kupelian, and Tom Ambrose at WorldNetDaily.com. Joseph, thanks for pestering me so many years ago to write a weekly column on the issues that matter most to our families and our future. I'll always be grateful to you for believing in me and for giving me a platform to encourage other parents. Through the pains and discipline of writing a weekly column, I actually came to love journalism. And to the folks at Townhall.com—especially Jon Garthwaite and Michael Spiller—who have supported and carried my column for more than two years, thanks very much.

Many thanks also go to my precious children—Drew, Nick, and Kristin—who have allowed me to share many of their stories.

Thanks, kids, for the lessons *you* have taught *me* and for the joy you bring to my life every single day. I love you with all my heart.

My deepest appreciation goes to my wonderful husband, Andy. Thank you for your love, support, feedback, and patience. You are my knight in shining armor, and I will forever love you with all that is within me. I'm so thankful that your parents raised you by God's standards rather than man's. Thanks Mamma and Papa John for instilling in Andy the qualities that make him a wonderful husband, father, and man of faith.

Musician Sara Groves, in her song "Generations," expresses what I remind myself of every day—and what I know is beating in the hearts of my co-workers and family, too:

> *Remind me of this with every decision,*
> *Generations will reap what I sow.*
> *I can pass on a curse, or a blessing,*
> *To those I will never know.*

Mom and Dad, America's heritage lives on, and yours does, too.

INTRODUCTION

The emerald green and turquoise waters, the soothing sound of waves crashing on the shore, the gentle breeze blowing through the hot summer afternoon—all these remind me of a simpler time when I used to vacation as a child on this quiet Florida beach. Seemingly untouched by our culture, this truly is an island paradise. On this trip, I have brought my three children and three of their friends. Because the only access to the beach is by boat, I feel we're safe here—safe from a culture that's gone stark raving mad.

Or are we? Is there any place in America where families are truly safe? Where children can grow up in innocence? Where moms and dads can know that it is their influence over their children's lives that will shape their values, choices, and futures? There was a time in America when parents raised their children with high morals, when adults instinctively created a protected space in childhood, free from exposure to "adult" issues. I fear that America is all but gone. Even here, on this beautiful, isolated island, the culture creeps. It creeps insidiously with the goal of invading the hearts and minds of our children and our families. One need only dial up on the Internet or turn on one of the hundreds of televisions connected to the satellite dishes that now adorn the roofs of virtually all of the beach houses to see the depths of depravity to which many Americans have become addicted over recent years—depravity that is robbing our children of their innocence and their future.

In my twenty years of marriage and seventeen years of being a mother, I've lived in glass and steel high-rises in the hustle and bustle of the city, on the outskirts of large metropolitan areas, and in the quiet cul-de-sac neighborhoods of suburban America. And in every single neighborhood, regardless of its proximity to a big city or its location relative to the country, still the culture creeps.

Millions of American families flock to cul-de-sac streets, envisioning them as safe havens in which to raise their children. Down on the circle at the end of the road, you don't have to worry so much about traffic. Your street is surrounded by houses owned by other families whose children join yours in playing safely—or so we imagine. The cul-de-sac street, so the legend goes, provides a quiet place for children to grow up with all the conveniences of the city nearby, yet protected from its dangers. On some level, we imagine the two-story homes, all nestled together in a circle, as the historic wagon trains of the Great West that encircled the fire at night providing safety for all the families, ready to fight off any outside forces who threatened the lives and dreams of the weary travelers. And while our modern house trains may provide some safety from vehicular traffic, statistics reveal the sad reality that a cruel enemy that attacks and often destroys the dreams of a better life has invaded even these neighborhoods.

Even the best of families have fallen victim to a *Home Invasion*—not by a pack of criminals who brazenly and forcefully assault us in order to rob us of our possessions, but by a culture that has slyly slithered into our senses in order to rob us of our souls.

Statistics now show that someone addicted to or peddling drugs may inhabit the picturesque home next-door or just down the street from you. In your own home, the enemy has likely invaded through the Internet, television, the radio, and even the books your children bring home from school. Our families are under attack 24/7, leaving many parents feeling helpless to protect their kids from a society that envelops them even in the "safety" of our own homes.

Just as any military officer will tell you that the worst place to fight an enemy is trapped in a cul-de-sac, so many parents are finding that they are now captives of an unrelenting enemy in their own homes, with no apparent escape. This omnipresent enemy that has overpowered our sensibilities and now holds America's families captive is a culture that has gone stark raving mad.

It's a heavy burden, but also a worthwhile endeavor, to be writing a book to share some of my stories, experiences, and successes in fighting the culture as a mother of three. I must admit at the outset that my efforts to combat the culture have not always been successful, nor have I always made the right choices. But I will say this: I arise each morning with a renewed commitment to pass on to my kids the morals and values in which my husband and I believe.

It is the right, the duty, the *privilege* of all parents to impart their own values to their children. We have a responsibility to arm our sons and daughters with sound principles and strong morals that will guide their lives and equip them to become the great parents and leaders of tomorrow. To do otherwise is to cheat them out of much happiness.

But too often, even good moms and dads, when confronted with the struggle—and believe me, it is a struggle—simply give up. They shrug their shoulders and decide, "I just don't have the energy to argue. Everybody's doing it, so what's the harm in my child doing it too?" This syndrome has become the mantra of far too many parents.

The purpose of this book is to encourage you to listen to that inner voice, that deep feeling that tells you something is amiss in the culture, and to act on it. Parents around the world are equipped with an instinct to protect their young—we know in our hearts basic truths about child-rearing and what characteristics are desirable in our kids. However, due to the constant onslaught of a culture that attacks basic moral principles and entices us to compromise, give in, and cast our good judgment aside, many of us have silenced our hearts through our own refusal to listen to what we *know* is true.

Far too often, parents thwart their protective instincts because of the peer pressure put on them by other parents who have long ago shrugged off the responsibility to follow that inner voice. I have received thousands of e-mails from moms and dads, grandparents too, over the several years that I have been writing my weekly column, "Heart Beat," for WorldNetDaily.com and Townhall.com. The common theme is often, "It's so hard to fight the culture. I know I need to do it; I just need help in knowing how."

Home Invasion will encourage you to stand up and protect

your children. Not by building walls that shut them off from everyone around them, but by building within *you* the strength of conviction and courage to raise your children with purpose, finding guidance from your own values rather than defaulting to those of a crazy world. In so doing, you will not only protect your children in the present, you will also raise them to become men and women of courage and conviction, with an unmistakable sense of who they are and what they believe.

I encourage you to seek out others who share your concerns but who may not have fully voiced them yet. Most parents, when they stop and think about it, don't want their children to be held captive by Hollywood, and MTV, and sexualized *everything*, and all the garbage that comes with it. Parents everywhere share the same concerns, but most just don't know where to turn for reinforcement and help. If you take the time and energy to look, to ask a few questions of other parents you know, you'll soon find that you are not alone in the battle even in your own neighborhood and school.

Although not heavy on statistics, *Home Invasion* contains enough facts to outline the overall problem and reveal the pervasiveness of the shallow mentality that would bring our children down to the lowest common denominator of humankind.

Also provided in this book are resources—help, *real* help that you as parents can call on to succeed in the battle for the hearts and minds of your children. They are arranged by subject matter and contain contact information and Web sites to help equip you and your family. Please use them.

Everyone knows, and history certainly shows, that children are best taught not by a list of do's and don'ts, but by example.

One of the first things I've had to do as I have become more aware of the battle and all that is at stake is to examine my example for my children. The first questions I have asked myself are, "In what are my values rooted? What are my personal morals? When is it okay to 'give in' or compromise, and on which issues do I stand firm? What is my source for personal strength and moral guidance? Do I make up the rules myself, or do I follow the rules set forth by a Higher Power?"

You must ask yourself these questions, too. I have chosen to follow the guidance of the Great Creator. The One that made us and loves us unconditionally also knows what is best for us, so why not follow His path? It's a great comfort to know that I don't have to reinvent the wheel or make it up as I go along. We can provide our children with no greater gift than to teach them that they have intrinsic worth—that God loves them, values them, and is there for them. To teach morality absent from God is to place on our children a burden they were never intended to bear—that of going it alone in a world that sends mixed messages about what is right, that constantly changes its definitions of truth. The basic guidelines—the two timeless truths we can teach our children to use as the marks by which to measure all decisions—are brilliantly simple, and incredibly powerful: "To love God with all your heart, and to love your neighbor as you love yourself."

The second step was to then look at my relationship with my spouse: "How do we model fulfillment, love, and happiness for our children? What media content do we consume on a daily basis? What kind of values and examples do we set for our children?" Long ago, my husband, Andy, and I took time to get it all out in the open and come to a common understanding of how we would proceed in protecting our family. I urge you to do the same—and to start today.

After examining my own source of faith, and then my husband and I recommitting to each other through a loving, selfless relationship where we face the world as a team, I discovered I had the proper framework in which to proceed. Suddenly, the issue of fighting the culture and the many daily battles, the daily questions, don't seem quite so hard anymore. The terms have been set, the guidelines have been determined, the roadmap has been laid out, and all I have to do is stay the course.

A special note to single parents: Although your challenge is harder, you can do it too, one day at a time, recommitting yourself to the cause every morning. It is essential that single moms seek out positive male role models for their children, and that single dads provide them with positive female role models. There's a reason why God designed the basic unit of society to include both a mother and a father—there are attributes and qualities unique to each gender that children benefit from. The manner and style in which a mother relates to her children are far different from how a father interacts with them—and our children need both influences to become well-rounded and have the best chance in life. Social science data proves men, women, and children are healthier, safer, better educated, more economically sound, more emotionally stable, and happier when they live with both a mother and father who share and model a loving relationship. But single moms and dads must not despair. By staying the course, filling in the gaps with trusted adults, choosing friends who affirm your values, and finding support within your church or community, your children can also rise above the status quo and become the adults of your dreams.

For all of us, there will be a crisis here and there—a bump in the road, a flat tire, an unexpected blown gasket, and you'll even run out of gas every now and then. But, with resources and reinforcement from others who share your values, with a reexamination on a daily basis of your commitment to your own beliefs, with a clear vision toward the future and the goal in mind of the kind of adult you want your child to become, it is obvious that the race is well worth the effort, and that you can chart your course and make it across the finish line in victory.

And isn't that what we all really want for our families and our children? To make it over the humps, to be successful through crisis, to learn how to make decisions that help us to be better people and protect our futures? Isn't that a lot better than giving in and giving up along the way?

There's not one parent reading this book that would consciously deny his or her children the ability to someday have their own loving, committed, fulfilling marriages, in which they are raising happy, loved children. In order to do that, *you* must resist the culture *now*.

Today's divorce rates hover around 50 percent. Hardcore pornography is rampant, and statistics show that even pre-school children have been exposed, through the Internet and television, to multiple images that debase and degrade humanity, that entice with the lie that many sexual partners leads to fulfillment. Teenage pregnancy rates are out of control, drug abuse is skyrocketing. Yes, Americans today are richer than at any point in our history. We have comforts and toys that most people around the world don't even know enough about to dream of. Yet ours is a culture also marked by unfulfilled lives, insatiable appetites, welfare dependency, lost dreams, fractured families, and broken hearts.

This dichotomy—this great American tragedy—is why ours must be the generation that seizes what remains of the day and fights a culture that has gone stark raving mad, largely fueled by a media world that is out of control.

This is not to say that you can't enjoy media and entertainment. Contrary to popular belief, the most successful movies are those that provide positive role models, noble messages, and show loving families, intact and strong. Believe it or not, it isn't the "slice and dice" and sex movies that people flock to, but those *are* the movies that are targeted to your kids. And Hollywood keeps producing more movies filled with more sexual and violent images geared toward younger and younger audiences. *Home Invasion* will encourage you to look beyond the catchy titles and cute little descriptions on the box to determine if the text really is appropriate for your four-year-old or teenager. Do you really want your child bombarded by sexual images, foul language, and graphic violence for violence's sake? My guess is, when you stop and think about it, the answer is *no*. Yet, every day, some parents are spending their hard-earned money to pay to have strangers come into their living rooms through television or video rentals to engage in sexual acts, use raunchy language, or commit acts of gruesome violence in front of their children. Intelligent moms and dads across the country actually sit their children on the couch, tell them to be quiet, and make them watch people engage in behavior on the tube that they wouldn't dare allow the actual actors to do live in front of their kids.

So *Home Invasion* is to encourage you to say, "I'm uncomfortable with this," and then turn it off. It's to help you to look beyond clever packaging or glossy movie reviews and see what's really there. It's to help you find others that share your values, who will join hands and hearts to "circle the wagons."

This book is about setting your family free from those who have invaded your home. It's about reclaiming your God-given role as the one who has the right, and the responsibility, to set the standards for your own precious children.

Invariably your children will go off to school, public or private, and come home with ideas presented to them that don't match your own. This book reminds you why, on a daily basis, it's crucial to find out what your kids are learning, to be involved in their education, and to insert and reinforce your own values into the teaching. It tells you where to find out what your rights are, as parents, in your state's public education system. It is possible to raise your children according to your values in the midst of a school system—but you must be engaged. *Home Invasion* will help you to reach out and encourage educators to think twice before just blindly following the curricula set forth, and to show appreciation to them when they stand for what is right and best for the children.

Please don't confuse the exercise of instilling timeless values and strong character into your children with that over-used phrase of "over-protecting" your kids. The early American pioneer parents taught their children about faith, loyalty, and purity. But they were also the most adventurous and daring parents in

America's history. They sought a better life for their families, and they sought it together—with immense courage. Protecting today's children from a modern culture that debases humanity and sexualizes every aspect of their lives will strengthen them from the inside out, and can afford them more opportunities for exploration and adventure as they grow into teens than their drifting counterparts. As you see your child developing into one who knows and appreciates limits and standards and principles, you will see a child that can be trusted to make decisions on his own at younger ages than his peers. You will find that as you see your child begin to self-govern based on a set of uncompromising standards, you will have to govern her less and less as she gets older. A higher level of personal independence is the blessing that both the parent and child enjoy when the child has developed and demonstrated that he has an internal moral compass and knows how to follow it.

So, moms, dads, grandparents, pastors, community leaders, teachers, this book is for you, it's for me—it's for all of us. It's to encourage us to draw that proverbial line in the sand, to reflect on the image of the wagons protectively encircling the fire to create a true safe haven for our children, and to do that in a real sense, in the modern culture. It's to protect our families, our children, and their futures. Why would we engage in this battle? Why would we take these bold steps? Because we love our kids. Because our children are depending on us to protect them. Because it's the right thing to do. And because we can win.

1

CULTURAL TERRORISM

Super Bowl 2004 has gone down in history as the most talked about Bowl of all time. Not because of the game, mind you. No, it was the halftime show, complete with Janet "Flashing" Jackson, that made it such an unforgettable experience for ninety million Americans—including my daughter and me. It now serves as perhaps the most infamous example of how our culture has gone stark raving mad.

There we were, my precious eleven-year-old and I, curled up on the couch anticipating a fabulous halftime extravaganza. Let's be clear about this: We weren't watching the game—not a single minute of it. Like most women I know, football just isn't my thing. But I'm also somehow connected to this event every year that seems to be the epitome of everything American. Besides, I've always enjoyed the creative commercials and halftime shows. Since all the guys in our family were watching the game elsewhere, I decided to make it a girls' night.

My daughter and I were having a blast running back and forth between decorating her room and trying to catch the much-awaited halftime spectacle. And boy, what a *spectacle* it was!

Halftime had already started before we realized it, so we

quickly scrambled to catch the rest of the show. Big mistake. I should have known better when I saw the cast of shady characters gyrating across the stage to chaotic music and words I couldn't quite understand. But I'm an optimist, so as Kristin and I snuggled close on the couch and threw the blanket over our legs, I just knew—or rather, nervously hoped—the show would get better.

"Besides," I thought, "millions upon millions of families are gathered around their television sets across America to watch the biggest show of the year—we can't all be wrong." At that precise moment, I became a very dumb blonde, relied on groupthink, ignored my inner instinct, and sat uncomfortably glued to the tube along with the rest of America and my trusting, vulnerable little girl.

By the time Justin Timberlake ripped off half of Janet's bra to reveal her bare breast as if she were some cheap lap dancer, it was too late.

But it wasn't just Janet's so-called "wardrobe malfunction" that made me regret tuning in. The crude over-sexualized commercials should have tipped me off that even the Super Bowl is no longer family-friendly. From crotch-grabbing dogs, to a monkey begging a girl for sex, to ads for medications promising to enhance romance, the nation was saturated with Super Bowl sex.

What exactly does any of that have to do with the American pastime of watching the biggest football game of the year? The attraction for so many millions used to be about the awesome display of teamwork, athletic ability, and strategy. It used to be about a competition between the best of the best. But America has been sliding down the slippery sewer of cultural immorality for so long that it was not until we were faced with the show's complete disregard for family values that we realized—ugh, we're covered with stinking sludge.

My friend, David Spady, of Salem Communications, has a much better phrase for what America was exposed to during that memorable Super Bowl Sunday: cultural terrorism. He's right. While American soldiers die overseas to protect our freedom, we're becoming slaves to malevolence in our own homes. While we're subjected to body searches at airports, increased monitoring of communications, and constantly changing terror alerts—all to combat terrorists who would destroy our nation—we *unwittingly* invite cultural terrorists into our homes under the guise of entertainment and education, and *unwittingly* allow them to destroy our sensibilities, personal values, and the innocence of our children. The American family is suffering from a home invasion that is robbing our children of their youth and their futures.

Moms, Dads . . . it's time to go to battle for our kids. Set the standards higher for your home, your schools, and yourselves. Set limits on everything from video content to television viewing to how your kids should dress—and stick with them. And let your voices be heard loud and clear by advertisers, networks, and others who would pass off moral depravity as family entertainment, "open-minded" learning, and "diversity." And join me in shutting off the smut . . . before it's too late.

A STEADY DIET OF GARBAGE

Another telltale sign of America's cultural degradation revealed in 2004 was the collection of now-infamous photos that were circulated around the world documenting the mistreatment of Iraqi prisoners by a few renegade American soldiers in Abu Ghraib prison. Every decent person I know reacted in horror to the story. When the lewd photos emerged of the "good guys" forcing prisoners to engage in sexual acts, and leading them around on leashes with hoods over their heads, and threatening them with electrocution, people were speechless and horrified.

We were right to be enraged and to demand that those involved be severely punished. And punished they were, including being discharged from the military and receiving prison time. Yes, our soldiers were in the midst of fighting the scum of the earth—terrorists. But the raunchy actions of a few renegade Americans in uniform temporarily caused us to lose the moral high ground in the war against evil. And although America did not forget that the vast majority of our brave soldiers are decent human beings who are willing to sacrifice their very lives to secure freedom for others, the unspeakable actions of a few put our military at great risk and caused our nation to be ridiculed.

Should we have been shocked that some Americans are capable of such barbaric behavior as depicted in the now infamous photos? Is it possible that the American culture aided and abetted this outrage?

Consider:

- Pornography is the No. 1 Internet industry—*No. 1.* According to 2003 statistics from the Internet Filter Review, there are 4.2 million porn Web sites.

- American consumers spent an estimated $220 million at such fee-based "adult" sites in 2001, according to Jupiter

Media Metrix, a New York Internet research firm. That was up from $148 million in 1999. Jupiter is projecting $320 million by 2005.

- A comprehensive two-year study by Alexa Research, a leading Web intelligence and traffic-measurement service, revealed "sex" was the most popular term for which people searched. According to their online searching habits, people want "sex" more than they want "games," "music," "travel," "jokes," "cars," "jobs," "weather," and "health" combined.

- A nationwide survey of 1,031 adults conducted by Zogby International and Focus on the Family on March 8–10, 2000, found that "20 percent of respondents—which extrapolates to 40 million adults—admitted visiting a sexually-oriented Web site. According to the Nielsen Net ratings, 17.5 million surfers visited porn sites from their homes in January of 2000—a 40 percent increase compared with September of 1999."

- According to *Time* magazine, pornographic images on the Internet increased by 1800 percent in the period from 1998 to the end of 2003.

- According to a 2001 report by the American Academy of Pediatrics Committee on Public Education, "American media are thought to be the most sexually suggestive in the Western hemisphere. The average American adolescent will view nearly fourteen thousand sexual references per year, yet only 165 of these references deal with birth control, self-control, abstinence, or the risk of pregnancy or STDs."

- The pediatric report also said that "56 percent of all programs on American television were found to contain sexual content. The so-called 'family hour' of prime time television (8:00 to 9:00 P.M.) contains on average more than eight sexual incidents, which is more than four times what it contained in 1976. Nearly one third of family-hour shows contain sexual references. . . . "

- According to The Medical Institute, "Several studies analyzing content of music videos showed that sexual intimacy was prevalent in 60–70 percent of them, there was an emphasis on sexual contact without commitment, and that 81 percent of videos that showed violence also showed sexual imagery."

- A study by the American Psychological Association found that exposure to sexualized violence is harmful, in particular in its effect on male attitudes about sex and intimacy, and causes males to be less sensitive to females.

- Graphic sex education is rampant in our schools, offering children as young as ten explicit demonstrations of contraceptive use (especially condoms) and direct encouragement to experiment sexually.

And that's just the tip of the iceberg.

The average soldier at the time the horrific events occurred in Abu Ghraib was receiving only three hours of training a year on the Geneva Conventions regarding the proper treatment of pris-

oners of war. Is it possible to deprogram and reprogram soldiers—
who come from a culture living the above-mentioned statistics—
in just three hours a year?

What about the rest of Americans—those of us who are not
in the military—who receive no formal training in how to treat
other human beings who are vulnerable? What is the future of
our country when our youth are feeding on a steady diet of
garbage?

Amid the noble struggle to establish and maintain a nation of
moral integrity, freedom, and faith in God, our history has also
included periods punctuated by acts of shame. The horrors of
slavery come to mind. Yet, almost alone among nations throughout history, the United States has always managed to hold herself
accountable for her ills, take corrective action, and move to a
higher level in our treatment of others.

Why? Because Americans once shared a collective understanding that ours is a society based on faith in God and His
immutable laws of unconditional love, decency, and the simple
but powerful concept of treating others as we would be treated.

Our schools once taught biblical principles. Our families
gathered regularly in churches and synagogues. Prayer was a standard part of life—both private and public. Americans were taught
the Ten Commandments and the rich Judeo-Christian heritage of
our country.

But all that changed in the 1960s when there began to be
a steady removal of God and His absolutes from the public
square. As a nation we forgot, as President Lincoln once said when
he quoted the Bible, "that the fear of the Lord is the beginning
of wisdom." Schools were purged of prayer and biblical values,

leaving a vacuum that was soon filled with the preaching of moral relativism, sexual anarchy, and a trashing of U.S. history. Now, about forty years later, there is no collective understanding of our Judeo-Christian heritage and the values that once permeated our halls of government, our schools, and our lives.

Our nation once looked to the truth of the book of Proverbs in the Bible: "To receive instruction in wise behavior, righteousness, justice and equity; to give prudence to the naïve, to the youth knowledge and discretion." Today, we teach our children to rely on their own wisdom and judgment formed by endless hours of sexualized programming, situational ethics, and group thinking. And we're surprised by the behavior of a few Americans at Abu Ghraib?

With the nonjudgmental, sex-crazed, anything-goes culture that we have become at home, it seems that America has set herself up for international humiliation and a dismal future. Our country permits Hollywood to put almost anything in a movie and still call it PG-13. We permit television and computers to bring all manner of filth into our homes. We permit school children to be taught that any type of sexuality should be viewed as an acceptable lifestyle. We allow Christianity and the teaching of Judeo-Christian values to be scrubbed from the public square. We allow our children to be taught how to use condoms in school, rather than why to avoid sex.

We let these things happen. They don't happen on their own.

It's time to take a cold, hard look at the degradation in our own country—and in our own homes. It's time to start protecting our families.

HOME INVADERS

Television's moral decline in programming and advertising; the rise of DVD players, VCRs, and the fall of ratings standards; and the ease of accessing hardcore pornography on the Internet make these media outlets the most dangerous of home invaders. For many legitimate reasons—entertainment, education, research, etc.—virtually every American parent has installed these easy routes for the enemy to infiltrate our homes. With the touch of a button or the click of the mouse, the vilest of human beings enter our living rooms and our children's bedrooms and engage in behaviors that we would never allow live, warm bodies to do. Yet, there they are—hour after hour, day after day—displaying their violence, graphic sex acts, and foul language in front of our children while good parents hang out in the kitchen and make dinner.

TV programming hasn't been truly safe for kids for at least twenty-five years. Oh, the process has been mostly gradual, of course. But to see how much things have changed, consider the fact that shows like *Three's Company*, *All in the Family*, and *Soap* were once considered very risqué. But today's prime time programming often makes shows filled "only" with sexual innuendo look tame.

The "family hour"—the time slot from about 8:00 P.M. to 9:00 P.M., when shows like *The Waltons*, *Little House on the Prairie*, and *Happy Days* used to air—is long gone. In its place we have culturally celebrated programs such as *Friends*, which ran for a decade, or, even more disturbing, *Will & Grace*. Yes, the writing in both of these shows is often clever and funny, but the normalization of rampant promiscuity and homosexuality is certainly not.

And these are just the most high-profile examples. "Think, for example, not just of the explicit raunchiness of MTV, but of the machine-gun double entendres of virtually every sitcom on television, aired and cabled all day long," Mitchell Pearlstein, president of Center of the American Experiment, noted in an article written as *Friends* was about to go off the air. "Now think of the near-impossibility of monitoring all of this and of maintaining age-appropriate moats around it."

And our kids are consuming this programming in alarming quantities. According to a 2001 report by the American Academy of Pediatrics Committee on Public Education, "[B]y the time adolescents graduate from high school, they will have spent fifteen thousand hours watching television, compared with twelve thousand hours spent in the classroom." This extrapolates to some three to four hours a day sitting in front of the tube. Of course, it doesn't help that many teenagers have a TV set in their rooms where they view anything they want, completely unsupervised— some 66 percent, according to a New York Times/CBS News poll.

And the problem doesn't stop with raunchy programs. There's not an hour in the day that is safe from ads laced with sex or violence. Many a parent who has carefully chosen a good program for the family to watch together must dive repeatedly for the remote control when an ad for, say, an R-rated movie or a sexual enhancement product pops up.

Even an ad that doesn't use suggestive or disturbing imagery or words can still prompt innocence-busting questions: "Mom, what's erectile dysfunction?"

Movie critic and national radio host Michael Medved is well acquainted with the power of visual imagery. As he and his wife, Diane, wrote in their book *Saving Childhood*, "Clicking on the remote control leaves children's impressionable minds open to any scene an advertiser or director wants to flash on the screen, and open to any belief system that will titillate an audience enough to increase profits."

Beyond the programs and the ads, we're saturated with 24/7 news programming that focuses on the sordid details of sex and/or violence stories from Lorena Bobbit to Monica Lewinsky, Scott Peterson to Mark Hacking. A study conducted by *U.S. News & World Report* and the Center for Media and Public Affairs "found that in 59.5 hours of coverage, the TV news operations ran 266 stories that by subject matter or on-air interpretations conveyed a sense of risk or peril—an average of 4.5 such stories per hour." The result, says Center Director Robert Lichter, is "an overwhelming portrayal of general misery. The overall picture is that America is in decline."

Worse, they often absorb these messages without a parent on hand to answer their questions and soothe their concerns. According to the Kaiser Family Foundation, children between the ages of two and seven watch TV without their parents present 81 percent of the time. Once they're over eight, kids watch without a parent 95 percent of the time. What good does a TV ratings system do, which just flashes a confusing jumble of letters like "TV-SV" up in the corner for a few seconds at the start of a show, when parents aren't there to act on it? Are the ratings designed simply to give producers a fig-leaf veneer of responsibility, as if to fool us into thinking that they care about our concerns?

Are you aware how much television your kids are watching? And what about the content?

SO WHAT?

In addition to making fatter kids who are wasting away thousands of hours of their childhood, the TV they're watching is also making them more promiscuous. Sexualized programming turns kids into sexually active children.

A September 2004 report in the medical journal, *Pediatrics*, says it all. I was actually a little shocked when my husband called me from work to say he had just opened the *Washington Post* to find the story detailing the report—and confirming what every parent knows in their gut must be true. The story said, in part:

"Teenagers who watch a lot of television with sexual content are twice as likely to engage in intercourse than those who watch few such programs." The article went on to quote Rebecca Collins, a psychologist with the Rand Corporation who headed the study, "This is the strongest evidence yet that the sexual content of television programs encourages adolescents to initiate sexual intercourse and other sexual activities. The impact of television viewing is so large that even a moderate shift in the sexual content of adolescent TV watching could have a substantial effect on their sexual behavior. The twelve-year-olds who watched a lot of sexual content behaved like the fourteen- or fifteen-year-olds who watched the least amount." Collins continued, "The advancement in sexual behavior we saw among kids who watched a lot of sexual television was striking." The *Post* story then said, "The study found that youths who watched large amounts of programming with sexual content were also more likely to initiate sexual activities short of intercourse, such as oral sex."

Now, don't you think it's time to listen to your inner instinct and help your kids change their viewing habits?

AND WHAT ABOUT "A NIGHT AT THE MOVIES?"

When I was a kid, selecting movies was pretty straightforward. Why? Because my parents had some hard and fast rules: G-rated movies were fine, but if the flick had a PG-rating, my folks were going to investigate it thoroughly before driving me to the theater to plunk down my two bucks. And R-rated movies? Forget it. They were strictly off-limits—as a matter of fact, no one I knew was permitted to go to R-rated movies. Those kids who snuck off in their teen years to do so were the talk of the school cafeteria.

So what about today? Most parents don't blink when even their very young kids want to take in a PG movie. And for many, PG-13 ratings are fine, too. But there's something most parents don't know: The standards for how movies are rated have changed drastically over the years.

A 2004 study of ratings and movie content by the Kids at Risk Project at the Harvard School of Public Health should be a wakeup call for parents who routinely allow their kids to see whatever the latest, hottest title is.

"The findings demonstrate that ratings creep has occurred over the last decade and that today's movies contain significantly more violence, sex, and profanity on average than movies of the same rating a decade ago," says the director of the project, Kimberly Thompson. It's a fact of life that the Motion Picture

Association of America (MPAA) has become increasingly lenient in assigning movie-ratings that are *supposed* to be "age-based."

The results of the study showed that there were significant "increases in violent content in films rated PG and PG-13, increases in sexual content in films rated PG, PG-13, and R, and increases in profanity in films rated PG-13 and R" than in the previous ten years.

In other words, this isn't your mother's PG-rating.

Simply put, today's PG movies are, in many cases, the R-rated movies of yesteryear. That means that parents who flip over the VHS or DVD box, see a PG-rating, and automatically deem it appropriate viewing are often deceived and may be quite disturbed at the actual content.

Even animated films have drastically changed over the years. The Harvard researchers found "a significantly higher amount of violence in animated films than in non-animated films." Thompson warns, "Given the possibility of long-term fear and anxieties from children's exposure to media, physicians should discuss media consumption with parents of young children and the fact that animation does not guarantee appropriate content for children."

Allow me to ask a few obvious questions: Why do physicians have to discuss media consumption with parents of young children? Why can't parents start taking a bit of the responsibility themselves? As much as I love pediatricians (my father was one and my brother-in-law is, too), shouldn't it be up to moms and dads to monitor what their kids are watching?

Thompson includes parental responsibility in her summary of the report, along with a warning about ratings in general,

"Parents and physicians should be aware that movies with the same rating can differ significantly in the amount and types of potentially objectionable content. Age-based ratings alone do not provide good information about the depiction of violence, sex, profanity, and other content, and the criteria for rating movies became less stringent over the last decade."

An e-mail one mom, Ginny, sent me in response to one of my WorldNetDaily.com and Townhall.com columns on movie content illustrates this point perfectly:

> My seven-year-old son's baseball coach gave him a movie to watch. "It is one of the best movies ever made," he said. I flipped it over and saw it was rated PG. I didn't think much about it, and my son watched it later that evening. The next evening, our family decided to watch the movie together. We began watching it, and I was slightly startled by the mature theme at times. But we kept watching. Then the screen was filled with a frontal zoom shot of a teenage girl's clothed breasts as she bounced down a sidewalk. The main character gawked. I looked at my husband, and he looked at me. We were both panic stricken. We stammered, I'm sure, and made up an excuse to stop watching the movie. I later looked up the movie review on PluggedInOnline.com and learned that the film also contains curse words that I found were very shocking for a PG movie.

Ginny continues:

> That movie changed my life. My heart ached that I had let my young son see the movie, and it made me realize that

there are many definitions of PG. It made me realize that my children should not see anything unless I first screen it. And it also made me realize that most of the world will try to tell you that it's "okay" to let our kids be part of this culture. I've found that many parents are just too lazy to protect their kids—and that they want to feel okay about their laziness at parenting, and if you're lazy too, it affirms them.

In other words, misery loves company. Ginny's children are very blessed. They have parents who are learning the cultural ropes, and listening to their instincts. They've resolved not to take the easy path of complacency and misery, but to, instead, truly *parent* their children.

WHO NEEDS PARENTS WHEN A CARD WILL DO?

And now there's the new "R-card." The GKC Theatre chain introduced something called an "R-card" in fall 2003 in Illinois and three other Midwest states. Its purpose: to give parents the ability to let their kids see R-rated movies without adult supervision.

Normally, anyone under seventeen can't get into an R-rated film without a parent or guardian. Several years ago, theater chains came under pressure from parents for not enforcing this rule very effectively, and they began insisting on forms of ID. But with the "R-card," young teens have blanket approval from their parents to see any R-rated film they please. Sure, the theater chain urges parents to give the kids the card only after approving a particular movie. But who are we kidding? Inevitably, kids will wind up seeing films they shouldn't—with no parent in sight.

As explained above, the MPAA movie ratings should never be the last word on which films are appropriate for children and teens to watch. Some movies that are given R-ratings contain no sexual material, but are given the rating because of violence. And sometimes—you probably won't believe I'm going to say this— movies rated R due to violence may actually be *appropriate* for some teens.

Consider two R-rated movies that both did well at the box office: *Halloween* and, more recently, *The Patriot*. The plot of a movie like any of those in the *Halloween* series is nothing but terror and bloody violence for violence's sake. These dumb movies deserve an R-rating.

In *The Patriot*, on the other hand, we follow the story of Benjamin Martin, who is drawn into fighting the British in the Revolutionary War after his son is killed. The film earned an R-rating, and properly so, for scenes of bloody violence during the fighting. Nevertheless, as in *Saving Private Ryan*, the violence was not employed for the sheer sake of titillating the audience; it was grounded in a moral universe in which the good guys—who were fighting to secure freedom—triumphed, and the oppressors were defeated. Such movies actually provide noble messages for teens about the importance of courage, and sacrifice, and of preserving liberty.

The bottom line is, parents should determine for each child in their household what is and isn't appropriate viewing. It's not enough anymore to go on the recommendation of a friend— unless you know that friend understands the cultural battle and is your partner in fighting it. And to make that determination, you've got to look beyond the ratings and the clever descriptions and reviews that are carefully chosen to lure you in. There are several great Web sites and resources to help you determine what you would have your child to see—I've listed a few of them in the Resources Section at the end of this book.

NO ESCAPE

Of course, those peddling harmful material often have a pat answer when parents complain: "Hey, don't blame us when kids go bad. We didn't put guns into the hands of the kids who decided to shoot up Columbine High School. The vast majority of kids who see our TV shows, movies, video games, etc., turn out fine. We're paid to *entertain*."

And so on. I'm sure you've heard many variations on this theme. The bottom line is Hollywood wants us to believe that "edgy" cultural material doesn't influence our kids at all. Of course, their actions belie their words. Are we supposed to believe that kids will be motivated, say, to care about global warming after they see *The Day after Tomorrow*, but won't conclude that sex outside of marriage is okay when they see it occur, consequence-free, in film after film? And do they really expect us to believe that advertising has no effect on the consumer when companies spend billions upon billions in advertising dollars every year?

In the name of "diversity," the cultural elite in Hollywood, in education, even some religious leaders, want us to believe that everything is okay, that no danger exists, that there is no such thing as depravity, and to say otherwise is to be judgmental. They believe that choice is everything—but that the range of choice must include everything the imagination can create. Of course, their hypocrisy is lost on them. Those of us who choose to provide a protective space of innocence for our children; who dare to define right and wrong; who seek to preserve traditional values of decency—well, we're just bigots who must be silenced.

The defenders of pop culture have another pat answer: "Change the channel. Nobody is forcing you to watch what we produce." In a 24/7 media culture, complete with cable systems boasting hundreds of channels, they've got to be kidding. Change it to what? Even if you pitch your TV out a window, declare the local multiplex off limits, and never buy another bad video game, your kids are hardly safe. And why? Because the products you're avoiding *still infect the overall culture.* And there's no changing the channel away from that. As *Time* magazine noted in an article about *Doom 3,* the sequel to the granddaddy of shoot-'em-up computer games, its makers "had created a three-dimensional virtual world so powerful, compelling, and disturbing that it would change the real world around it." The same can be said about many other games, as well as a slew of dark or raunchy TV shows, CDs, and movies.

One of Michael Medved's favorite experiments when he's giving a lecture is to ask the audience, "How many people have been to a Madonna concert?" Maybe two or three hands go up out of group of several hundred. "How many have bought a Madonna CD?" A few more hands go up. "How many of you know who Madonna is?" Every hand goes up. "Now, how many of you *choose* to know who Madonna is?" Everyone laughs. But that's the key: You didn't choose. It was forced on you by the larger culture.

As Medved puts it, "I guarantee you there are Amish kids in Pennsylvania who ride in buggies and don't use zippers who know who Madonna is!"

Other times, critics try to belittle our concerns. When Bill Maher, host of HBO's *Real Time*, recounts how he unwittingly broke an unwritten taboo by saying "sucks" on *The Tonight Show* in 1983, he adds that "three days later, Johnny [Carson] said it. I had stupidly, naively tested the waters, and the dam didn't break. Nobody called; the world didn't come to an end." He's wrong, though. Such milestones may be small, but they add up, and pretty soon, one world *has* come to an end—the world of innocence for even the youngest of children.

FREE SPEECH?

I, for one, have had enough. Janet Jackson and her ilk have effectively declared war on America's families, and it's time to fight back. It's been encouraging to see the Federal Communications Commission finally cracking down on indecency in the wake of Janet Jackson's Super Bowl appearance. During the first half of 2004, the FCC leveled more than $2.5 million in fines against broadcasters. As a special "culture wars" report in *Entertainment Weekly* magazine notes, that's more than the proposed fines over the previous decade *combined.*

But how are broadcasters reacting? Some have made some welcome changes, but others are fighting back and vowing to protect "free speech." *Entertainment Weekly* flagged a few of the shows they were planning to unveil in fall 2004, including *Life As We Know It,* a "teenage boink-a-thon that features a student engaging in X-tracurricular activities with his teacher"—one of a number of shows relying on sex to sell themselves. Even in *7th Heaven,* an originally (and deliberately) wholesome show, "college-age Simon will become the first Camden kid to say yes to premarital sex."

In 2004 I attended one of the largest annual events of the powerful talk-radio industry. "Talker's 2004" had as its theme, "The Last Stand for Freedom of Speech?" Front and center was the fact that the FCC had cracked down (a little) on a few "shock jocks." The keynote address was delivered by one of these trash-talkers who spent some thirty minutes or so claiming that the First Amendment is at risk because he can't say "f—k" on the air. I kid you not. Forget the fact that the airwaves are public property, forget the fact that kids might be listening, forget the fact that decent adults don't want their sensibilities assaulted when they're scanning the radio in the car, forget the fact that the framers of the Constitution never intended for every kind of speech to be protected in every situation. Ever heard of libel laws? Or how it's illegal to slander someone? Ever try to yell "fire" in a crowded building? Some things are just not acceptable under the banner of "free speech," and among them is indecency.

NO OUTCRY

So although Americans followed their instincts and expressed outrage at what happened during Super Bowl 2004, expect things to get worse—not better. The majority of Americans are not willing to fight the status quo for any length of time. But the opposition—the mass marketers—is in the battle for the long haul, and it is determined to win.

Bill O'Reilly, noted author, former teacher, radio talk show host, and star of the wildly popular Fox News program, *The O'Reilly Factor*, on which he works to better America every day, summed up the cultural problem this way one evening in his "Memo" segment:

The belief that America is degenerating on a moral level is shared by both Republicans and Democrats. According to a new Gallup poll, 82 percent of Republicans and 78 percent of Democrats say that moral values in the U.S.A. are only fair or downright poor. Forty years ago, only 33 percent of Americans felt that way.

So what's happened? First, secular forces have destroyed any rendering of Judeo-Christian philosophy in the public school system. Many teachers are now ordered not to make value judgments on behavior and not to push any specific moral standards. Thus, children receive little if any moral guidance in class.

Second, with the rise of single-parent homes, more and more American kids wind up unsupervised for long periods of time, left to the television set or the computer, where harmful material comes at them like rain in a thunderstorm.

Third, major corporations now traffic in sex and violence to an extent never before seen in this country. Americans spend more than ten billion dollars a year on porn. And violent video games gross billions more for corporations.

Fourth, peer pressure to actually reject immoral behavior is virtually nonexistent in many places. The military criminals at Abu Ghraib never could have committed their crimes if other soldiers did not look away. The code of silence about bad behavior is an infectious disease among Americans.

He continued,

Millions of American parents are trying hard to teach their children good values but are besieged by the terrible influences beyond the home. The secularists have succeeded in drastically changing the moral tone in this country. And 80 percent of us see that change as a bad thing.

However, there's no mass outcry about it. And until there is, America will continue its declining moral direction.

Bill is right. Only if decent Americans learn to voice their opinions, stay the course, and incorporate a few common sense practices into their daily lives can we hope to protect our families from the madness. No one is immune from the effects of our immoral culture—we can all slip up and make mistakes. But the point is, when we fail, we must vow to continue moving in the right direction.

My daughter accompanied me when I interviewed Bill in New York for this book. Even at her tender age of twelve, she wondered why, if people aren't happy with the moral direction our nation is headed, we don't stop it. Bill expressed his thoughts on the problem:

The polling numbers show that people are for self-reliance, a small, fair government, have a spiritual outlook on life, and want their kids taught values. But today a lot of parents are lazy. The baby boomers tend to be lazy, self-absorbed parents—and if you're going to be a lazy parent, then your kids will be exposed to garbage and a lot of emotional stuff they aren't ready for, and, as a result, will be damaged individuals.

When I asked him about the school's role in the cultural decline he responded,

Teachers are afraid to say certain things are morally wrong—they're afraid kids will tell their parents and the parents will complain. So many teachers do nothing in the arena of teaching values—combine that with the fact that many parents just aren't around anymore because they're too busy with their own lives, and you see the problem. Too many kids get no moral guidance at home or at school, but the media pushes garbage 24/7. Children need strict parental guidance, and when they have parents that think it's okay for ten-year-olds to watch R-rated movies filled with sex and violence and listen to music that glorifies dope dealers, you get kids that will fail and become part of the problem.

Kristin listened intently and it all made sense to her.
Doesn't it make sense to you, too?

ASLEEP AT THE SWITCH?

It seems that nearly every American, post 9/11, pointed a finger at the CIA, the FBI, recent presidents, and others for being "asleep at the switch"—for failing to take action when all the signs indicated that America was about to be attacked by terrorists on our own soil.

How are we, as moms and dads, taking action against the home invasion by cultural terrorists who are attacking our families on every front? Are we, too, asleep at the switch?

Maybe the battle to protect your family's morality seems too hard. Maybe you feel you don't have enough support. Will it take some personal catastrophic event in your kids' lives to galvanize you into action? Will it be too late?

The evidence is all around us. The enemy has invaded our homes, and it's time to throw the bums out.

When in the thick of writing this book, I received an e-mail from one reader of my weekly column that shows how she threw the bums out of her home:

> My husband and I recently saw a change come over our eleven-year-old honor student. Up to this time she had been respectful, intelligent, and enthusiastic. We made the mistake of giving her her own television with minimal supervision, and this child turned surly, disrespectful, and apathetic about EVERYTHING. We shipped her off to her grandparents (former military) for the summer, and when she returned, the TV was gone as were any and all CDs we considered inappropriate, etc. The end result is

we have gotten our sweet, smart, respectful daughter back, and she now realizes what an effect all that trash was having. Hard lesson for us and her—but one we won't make with her younger siblings.

Media critic and veteran radio host Bob Just wrote in the December 2003 edition of *Whistleblower* magazine:

> Increasingly, the horror of America's culture is becoming frighteningly clear, both for its evil intent and for its devastating effect on the nation's children. We see it everywhere, and most of us feel helpless. We live in a child-molesting culture that is destroying the character and moral core of our nation—and that has targeted our kids.
>
> The culture war that is going on in America is nothing less than a battle for your child's mind. At heart, it's an "identity war" (including gender identity) that can leave your child lost, frustrated, alone—and perhaps permanently so.
>
> Don't kid yourself. This issue is a matter of life and death. And not just because of drugs, or AIDS. There is the slow death of betrayal, anger, despair, lost opportunity, and broken dreams.

Moms, Dads, I ask you: *Who will shape your child's identity?*

2

SEXUALIZED EVERYTHING

Barreling down Interstate 95 from our home in Virginia for a relaxing family vacation on the beach in Florida, I found myself wondering how in the world things got so bad. I-95 runs from Maine all the way down to central Florida. It's the most direct driving route to the ultimate family vacation destination: Disneyworld. The problem is, you can't reach the childhood fantasy-land without first traveling down miles of highway littered with tacky billboards promising adults a very different type of fantasy.

As I hit North Carolina, I found myself trying to divert the attention of my kids and their friends away from the garish sexual signs. Travelers are literally bombarded by colossal billboards screaming, "Topless! Topless!" and "We Dare! We Bare!" How on earth did we ever permit our culture to become so consumed with sex that a family can't even drive down the highway without having their children attacked by raunchy sex ads?

Once in South Carolina, we decided to exit the highway to fill up on gas, stretch our legs, and grab a snack. I was delighted to discover that the gas station we picked was one of those combo convenience stores with a Baskin-Robbins located inside where I could get a scoop or two of my beloved Rocky Road ice cream. While I stopped off at the restroom, my twelve-year-old daughter and her friend and my two teenage boys and their friends surrounded the counter to place their orders. By the time I joined them, I wished I had gotten there sooner.

To my dismay, sitting on a rack right at eye level by the register where the kids were paying for their ice cream cones was a display featuring a product called "Horniest Goat Weed," described in bold letters on the front of the box as "Sex stimulate pills for men and women." So a kid can't even get a scoop of ice cream without being subjected to a sex message? The kids dispersed from the counter while I stepped up to finish paying the bill. When I turned around, my girls were standing at the magazine rack next to some creepy, middle-aged guy who was flipping through a porn magazine. Once again, I found myself diverting the attention of my kids. Good grief. Time to hit the road.

As we continued down the highway through Georgia and Florida, the landscape was again trashed by billboards screaming, "Café Risque—24 Hour Adult Café" and "We Bare All!" and "Adult Toys." It seems these cheap, dumpy topless bars that now dot the countryside bring in enough business these days to pay for scores of trashy billboards up and down the highway for miles and miles. This sad reality points out two truths: the high level of immorality of many adults and the fact that their "choices" do affect others—even little kids on their way to Disneyworld.

THESE ADULTS TODAY

My family is well known by our friends for taking what are known as legendary Hagelin road trips: One trip a couple of years ago was composed of two adults, six children (three of them friends of my children), a dog, a van, and twenty hours of highway. Both ways.

We get a lot of camaraderie out of such trips. We rinse off a lot of sand. We go through a lot of suntan lotion. And we eat a lot of food you won't find on the surgeon general's recommended list anytime soon. Sometimes, we nearly kill each other, but, all in all, these family trips are loads of fun and are filled with the stuff great memories are made of.

On this particular trip, we stopped in a chain burger joint—one of the biggies—and were eating when I noticed a made-for-television movie playing on a mounted television in the corner. As I watched, the characters began removing their clothes and, in very short order, were into some pretty heavy romping.

"Grab your food, kids," I said. "We have to go."

Less than a week later, a friend told me about an astoundingly sexual fragrance ad in *Teen People* magazine. Not wanting to believe what he said, I headed to the grocery store to check out the magazine myself. There it was, in living color on the checkout stand. I picked up the magazine, and it flipped open to the ad in question. It featured a young, shirtless teen boy snuggled up next to a teen girl clad only in her underwear. The two were posed cozy and playful on a bed, with the caption, "Scent to bed." The name of the fragrance? "Fcuk you."

The letters are not-so-cleverly rearranged, and their meaning is obvious. On the back of the page are two fragrant strips: one says, "open here to try fcuk her" and the other, "open here to try fcuk him." A quick scan of the articles in the magazine proved to be a parent's worst nightmare. Almost everything is linked to sex. It broke my heart when I turned to the "letters from readers" page and saw that girls as young as twelve and thirteen are regular readers of the magazine.

Everywhere I turn, I have to fight for my kids' character, if not their souls. And it's getting worse every day. From the movie theater to the grocery checkout line to the burger joint, the people in my generation—the adults who ought to know better—keep flinging garbage at America's children.

Have we gone stark raving mad?

The problem isn't with "These kids today!" The real problem is with "These adults today!"

We adults have messed up big time. We produce the rotten movies and television programming, and we put up the big bucks for publications. We adults create the marketing plans, write the lyrics, take the photos. All for the sake of the almighty dollar.

And it's our children who are paying the price.

The sexual images that pummel them also promise popularity, security, acceptance—all those things on which teens feed. And it's all a bag of vicious lies. As my colleague at The Heritage Foundation, researcher Robert Rector, points out, teen sex leads to deadly STDs, unwanted pregnancies, and lost futures—and also to increased depression, lowered self worth, and increased possibility of suicide.

Because preteens as a group now spend millions of dollars every year, adults are targeting kids with graphic sexual images at younger and younger ages. Recent research shows an increasing amount of sex-oriented marketing aimed at children in what psychologists call the "latency period." This is the period before full puberty when boys and girls find each other "yucky," when they form their own identities unburdened by the need to impress the opposite sex. They need to be left alone, not encouraged to "get with it."

Yet, we take their innocent, pliable, trusting young minds and allow others to destroy them each time we let them watch garbage while we look the other way. Often, our reaction is to simply shrug our shoulders in indifference at the cultural sewage.

But how can we be indifferent when our children are at risk? According to a February 2004 report by Advocates for Youth, some 50 percent of the new cases of sexually transmitted diseases in our country occur in young people from fifteen to twenty-four years old. Gonorrhea and chlamydia have risen in the same group by more than 50 percent. The group estimates that one in two of sexually active teens will become infected with an STD before they are twenty-five years old.

"The increasing portrayals of sex in movies and television programs have had a tremendous negative effect on our children," says Ted Baehr, publisher of *Movieguide*. "Some media pundits and politicians think that such programming is inconsequential and has nothing to do with our children's future. That response is ignorant and wrongheaded."

FEEDING THE FIRE

My husband was listening to NPR's *This American Life* one day and nearly ran off the road when he heard a story filed by reporter Ira Glass, who had decided to take a look at the American high school phenomenon known as "the prom."

Now, even when I was in high school, there were wild stories about what some kids did after the prom. Let's face it: the high school years have long been marked in modern America by tales of kids who decide to use prom night as their night to "go all the way." Most of it, until recent days, has been urban legend. Even so, what has drastically changed over the years is the role some adults—the chaperones—play at proms and dances. Adults are present at such functions for one reason: to be chaperones, to make sure the environment is safe and that kids don't get out of hand. Somewhere along the way, some adults have gone from protecting our kids from hormonal tendencies to actually encouraging behavior that only feeds the fire.

Here's an excerpt from the transcript of the NPR story that nearly sent my husband spinning:

IRA GLASS: On the dance floor there was a certain amount of copping feels and kissing. But the sexual tension of the prom hit a kind of surreal zenith when the deejay told the boys to bring chairs down to the dance floor—the girls were seated in the chairs—and the garter ceremony began.

EMCEE AT DANCE: We will count down on ten.

GLASS: Over a hundred teenage girls presented bare legs with garters.

EMCEE: All hands—you have to put your hands behind your back.

GLASS: Meaning, grab the garter with your teeth.

EMCEE: All right. I'm going to count backwards from ten. Ten, nine, eight . . .

GLASS: This is the kind of activity that separates the "just-friends" prom dates from the real dates. And dozens of just-friends stood around the edges of the hall in various states of discomfort. [Countdown continues in background.] A hundred kneeling teenage boys bring their faces up against the slightly sweaty thighs of their dates, grip multi-colored garters with their teeth, and drag them off their legs. It's a shocking and amazing sight. But when I ask teachers about it later, they all say, "Where have you been? They've done this for years!" At homecoming, apparently, things get even more explicit.

EMCEE: Okay, let's move the chairs, and we'll have a slow dance.

Do our kids have a chance when adults are egging them on?

According to recent research, our children are paying—with their bodies—for the sins of their parents, who shed their own morals during the sexual revolution of the seventies and are passing on their brand of immorality through the media, education, and the culture in general.

In one survey by the National Campaign To Prevent Teen Pregnancy, it was revealed that almost 20 percent of children have had intercourse before their fifteenth birthday. One in seven of these sexually active girls became pregnant. Having sex at such an early age leads to many problems, the study noted. Sexually experienced children were far more likely than virgins to engage in other risky behavior. They were six times more likely to drink at least once a week. They were three times more likely to smoke and four times more likely to use marijuana.

Yet, still the media feeds the lie that engaging in sex should be a way of life for our kids. Even those TV viewers who consider themselves big fans of the teen soaps—once *Beverly Hills 90210*, now *The Mountain* and *The OC*—must have realized that something about the way those shows depicted sex just didn't ring true.

The "cool" kids, the kids everyone wanted to be like, were the ones who "did it." Supposedly, they were tough enough and strong enough to have sex and then walk away. They were able to "do it" for "its" sake. They didn't have to get involved in the maw of personal commitment, love, and sharing. No, they could take their gratification and run, and they allegedly were better for it.

Of course, this didn't quite square with what I'd seen when I was that age, nor with what I see now among my children's contemporaries. Those who dared didn't come back emboldened. They came back saddened. Disappointed. Less trusting in themselves and of others.

SEX, SADNESS, AND SUICIDE

The sad anecdotal stories we've all seen are backed by equally sad statistics in a report by The Heritage Foundation. Researchers Lauren Noyes, Kirk Johnson, and Robert Rector compiled data that show sexually active teens are far more likely to be depressed and to attempt suicide than those who hold off until marriage.

Using results from the National Longitudinal Survey of Adolescent Health, conducted for the National Institute of Child Health and Human Development and seventeen other federal agencies, the Heritage study reveals that more than a quarter of teen girls who said they were sexually active also said they had been depressed "a lot of the time" or "most or all of the time" in the previous week, compared to 7.7 percent of girls who said they weren't sexually active.

More tellingly, 60.2 percent of girls who refrained from sex said they were "never or rarely" depressed, compared to just 36.8 percent of sexually active girls. For boys, 8.3 percent of those who were sexually active reported problems with depression, compared to just 3.4 percent for those who weren't.

The in-home survey (given with parental permission) of sixty-five hundred people ages fourteen to seventeen years old also asked if they had attempted suicide during the past year. Girls who were sexually active were three times more likely to say they had attempted suicide than those who weren't. Sexually active boys were nearly nine times more likely to have attempted suicide.

One could raise a chicken-and-egg argument here. Does sex cause depression, or does depression cause sex? And don't some kids in unhappy homes use sex to escape depression? But as the Heritage analysis points out, the differences in happiness between sexually active and non-sexually active kids are too large and too widespread for the depression to have caused the sex in most cases.

These kids with troubled homes could've lashed out in any number of ways. Also, a majority of teens that had become sexually active admitted they'd started too soon and expressed regret. Advocates of "safe sex"—those with the harebrained idea of giving away condoms at school—must face the fact that there is no condom for the brain or heart. For them, the only negative consequences of teen sex they seem to care about are the physical dangers (and even then, with the high failure rate of condoms, kids are never fully protected from either disease or pregnancy).

What about the emotional and psychological dangers?

Rector explains that the consequences of teen sex are felt for a lifetime: "Sexual activity by teens has both short-term and long-term negative psychological effects. It disputes their ability to develop loving, intimate, and committed relationships and thereby creates great unhappiness in later life."

The only way to truly protect kids from damaging their complete health is to teach them to wait. You can never tell what will catch a kid's attention. Some may not fear pregnancy or sexually transmitted diseases. For them, maybe these findings will turn their heads, and they'll learn that, contrary to the commercials and the TV shows and everything else that screams at them to have sex now, sex doesn't make you happy and, in fact, can make you fatally sad.

A CULTURE OBSESSED WITH PORN

The horrible reality is that ours is a culture obsessed with sex. Sexual images are everywhere. And they aren't just of men and women having sex. There are adults with kids, kids with kids, group sex, sex with animals—anything goes. The images that have invaded our homes are degrading, debasing, and desensitizing all of us.

In 2004, *World and I* magazine published a report I wrote on the prevalence and dangers of pornography in America. But I wasn't the first one to talk about it. In November of 2003, *60 Minutes* aired a piece by Steve Kroft on the mainstreaming of the pornography industry. He attended a porn "trade show," talked with porn stars and those who market their "work," exposed the companies of surprisingly high stature that now profit from smut, and explored just how pervasive the industry has become.

The venerable CBS news magazine jumped in the ratings from twenty-first the previous week to second the week Kroft's report appeared.

From the Internet, with its a la carte offerings of porn for every pervert, to the hotel/motel industry, which does a tidy business selling in-room blue movies to guests, to the neighborhood video rental stores, porn—which seemed to be dying a slow death as recently as fifteen years ago—has become a booming business.

Consider: Sex is the No. 1 topic searched for on the Internet. Gambling is second.

Americans spend ten billion dollars per year on porn, as much as they spend on sporting events or movies or music. Paul Fishbein, founder and president of *Adult Video News* magazine and promoter of the show Kroft attended, said there are eight hundred million rentals each year of adult videotapes and DVDs.

Of course, literature that could be classified as hardcore porn has existed for centuries. And hardcore porn movies have been around almost as long as film itself. According to Ed Halter, writing for *Village Voice*, today's stars with porn in their past, such as Pamela Lee Anderson and Paris Hilton, are following a trail blazed by, among others, Joan Crawford, Marilyn Monroe, and Chuck Connors.

But in recent years, porn availability has exploded, particularly on the Internet. Today, well over one thousand U.S.-based firms operate more than one hundred thousand subscription porn Web sites, and some two hundred thousand other sites freely give out the garbage to anyone who knows the Web address or happens to stumble across it while searching the Net. Two-thirds do not even warn about their adult content, and only three percent require viewers to prove they are adults before entering. Three in five searches conducted on the Net in the United States are to seek out porn, according to a study published in the *Washington Times*.

Child porn—which is illegal to create worldwide—continues to grow as well. The FBI pursued about seven hundred cases of child porn in 1998; by 2001, it was pursuing more than twenty-eight hundred. Demand for pornographic images of babies and toddlers is "soaring," according to Professor Max Taylor, who has documented efforts to fight pedophilia information networks in Europe. Approximately twenty new children and twenty thousand new images of child porn are posted on the Internet each week, experts have said.

The U.S. Customs Service estimates that one hundred thousand Web sites offer child pornography, more than half of which originate in the United States.

As the numbers have grown, so has the variety of acts depicted. Virtually every imaginable fetish is addressed. As Dennis Hof, an associate of *Hustler* magazine publisher Larry Flynt, told the *New York Observer*, "You've got Larry and [*Penthouse* publisher Bob] Guccione doing things that ten years ago, you'd go to prison for. Then you've got all this Internet stuff—dogs, horses, twelve-year-old girls, all this crazed Third-World s— going on."

How did this happen? How did the number of movies produced each year increase tenfold in a decade? How did such mainstream companies as Hilton and Marriott, General Motors and Time-Warner become leading—if not proud (don't, for instance, look for listings of the porn profits in their annual reports)—purveyors of smut?

The reason is simple: Despite all the new players in the market, porn remains enormously profitable. According to the *60 Minutes* report, DirecTV, owned by Hughes Technology, a subsidiary of General Motors, pulled in five hundred million dollars from adult entertainment in 2002. Comcast, the nation's largest cable company, made fifty million. All the nation's top cable operators—from Time-Warner to Cablevision—distribute sexually explicit material.

To the nation's top hotel chains—Hilton, Marriott, Hyatt, Sheraton, and Holiday Inn—smut can mean the difference between red and black ink on the ledger. The *60 Minutes* report said that half the guests in these hotels order in-room adult movies and that these orders account for nearly 70 percent of their profits.

SO WHAT'S THE HARM?

It's now undeniable that considerable harm can come from long-term porn abuse. In just the last five years, organizations have proliferated to help people who feel a compulsive "addiction" to pornography. Pornography—by itself, not as part of an accusation of adultery—has begun to arise with what Jenkins calls "alarming frequency" in divorce and custody proceedings.

"The more accessible the material, the larger number of people who will be willing to consume it because they can do so discreetly," Jenkins said in a February 2001 article for *Policy Review* magazine. "The larger and more scalable the market, the more it can supply material to dovetail with every individual quirk or taste. Given the way porn seems to act on those who are most susceptible to it, we may be surprised at the results."

Jenkins pointed to Dr. Mark Laaser, a co-founder of the Christian Alliance for Sexual Recovery who is himself a recovering "sex addict." Citing recent research, Laaser says just as alcoholics build up tolerance and must then drink more to receive the same effect, sex addicts—because of naturally occurring chemicals in the brain—also build up tolerance and need more input for the same satisfaction. The National Council on Sexual Addiction Compulsivity estimates that 6 to 8 percent of Americans are sex addicts.

"I have treated one thousand male and female sex addicts," Laaser told Congress in 2002. "Almost all of them began with pornography."

They begin with "soft" pornography and move through four stages to sexual addiction, according to Dr. Victor Cline, an expert on the topic. They start by using porn for an aphrodisiac, followed by sexual release. From that, they move to escalation, in which they require more explicit and deviant material to meet their needs. As this progresses, a third stage—desensitization—takes hold, as material that once was perceived as gross, shocking, and disturbing becomes common and acceptable.

Finally, for some, this leads to acting out sexually the behaviors viewed in pornography, which leads, for men, to a dehumanization of the women in their lives. This partially explains why Phoenix police found that neighborhoods where adult businesses were located had a 43 percent higher rate of property crimes and a 4 percent higher rate of violent crimes. It almost fully explains the 506 percent increase in sex crimes.

For these men, sexual gratification begins to overwhelm all other desires. According to the National Coalition against Pornography, they come to view sex solely as a vehicle for their own physical pleasure. They come to see it as an act without consequence with a person who doesn't matter, and they view marriage and sound relationships as barriers to happiness. This leads to breakdowns in relationships and often divorce.

Porn drives some to engage in behaviors they previously had managed to hold in check. For instance, in a study of convicted child molesters, 77 percent of those who molested boys and 87 percent of those who molested girls admitted to the habitual use of pornography in the commission of their crimes. They use porn to stimulate themselves, to illustrate to victims what they want them to do and to break down the inhibitions of children—to try to convince them it's okay because, look, this kid is doing it, and his mommy isn't mad, and it's fun because, look, this kid is enjoying it.

Thankfully, nearly all children are reluctant to take part in such activities. They don't understand—as an adult would—why this kind of touching is improper. But they know it is, they recoil when it happens, and they're never again comfortable around that adult. This is why experts on child sex abuse and child porn invariably tell parents to pay attention when their children are wary of a particular adult.

THE DANGER OF CHAT ROOMS

The Internet not only brings porn into the home where people can view it in private but also removes the age restriction. As a result, nine out of ten children ages eight to sixteen who have Internet access have viewed porn Web sites, usually while looking up information for homework assignments, according to a study by the London School of Economics.

With the Web, it's not just porn sites that present a problem; it's e-mail and chat rooms as well. Stories of adults who lured children into porn or sexual abuse through the Internet are too numerous to mention. A "friend" appears in an otherwise harmless chat room. A relationship forms. A meeting is arranged.

This is where the problem gets really out of hand. A survey for the Kaiser Family Foundation found that 90 percent of teens and young adults have access to e-mail, and half check their inbox at least once a day. Three out of four have access at home, and nearly one in three can access e-mail from their own rooms, unsupervised by parents.

According to the National Center for Missing and Exploited Children, two out of five missing children ages fifteen to seventeen are abducted due to Internet activity. You get a picture of how huge the problem is getting when you understand that the FBI reports that three kids are reported missing into the FBI's computer program system *every two minutes of every day.*

One of my great privileges is to serve as a volunteer on the Advisory Committee for Web Wise Kids, a nonprofit organization dedicated to protecting children from online predators. The founder of Web Wise Kids was inspired to begin the organization because her own fourteen-year-old sister disappeared for four months after an in-person meeting with an adult male she had been chatting with online. Although her sister was rescued, most kidnapped children aren't. This horror is occurring more and more every day, with middle school children being particularly vulnerable because they spend so much time on the Internet. Of the forty-five million children who have Internet access, over 50 percent say they have been contacted by a stranger in a chat room or through e-mail.

The trouble is, most children never tell their parents that they chat with strangers, because kids love the mystery and don't want to be restricted from using their computers. Parents, you must take action to protect your kids *today*, whether you have online access in your home or not. Your children will use the Internet—at home, at friends' homes, in school, at the library, somewhere. It's up to you to teach them to be safe. Here are a few practical tips that you can start doing today:

- Computers must never be set up in a child's room. Put your system in a common area where activity can be more closely monitored, like a living room or kitchen. Never allow your child to access the Internet behind closed doors.

- Buy an Internet filter. There are several great ones—I happen to use the American Family Association's filter (available at www.AFA.org). There is a charge, but it is well worth the money to protect your kids.

- Don't let your kids go to chat rooms or talk endlessly online through instant messaging. Even with friends, the conversations get out of hand. Kids are more likely to use crude language or delve into personal areas when they talk online than they are in person. And you never know who is watching or listening in such a group setting. Just say no to such situations.

Web Wise Kids teaches children how to make their online experiences safe and fun through the use of "Missing," an educational CD-Rom and computer detective game. The adventure contains many of the scenarios most frequently used by predators in chat rooms with kids—the tricks that lure many children to great harm. It's a fun, interactive game that helps kids recognize the signs of online "friends" who could be deadly. You can get the game at www.WebWiseKids.com—kids love to play computer games, and this one just may save their life.

The bottom line is, as Web Wise Kids explains on its site, "Today's technology offers wonderful and amazing potential, but there is a dangerous side and we need to learn how to use this marvelous new tool sensibly. Kids are being confronted with situations and materials beyond their years. They need to be equipped to handle choices wisely."

And the only one who can equip them is . . . you.

3

MANIPULATING MINDS
FOR MONEY

Marketers are out to get America's youth, and they'll stop at nothing to do it.

Parents take note: The only thing that stands between your kids and those who seek to exploit them for the sake of the almighty dollar is *you*.

The average child sees some twenty thousand advertisements each year, according to New Strategist Publication's "Getting Wiser to Teens: More Insights into Marketing to Teenagers." By the time a child reaches age nineteen, they will have seen some three hundred thousand placed ads. And those are just easily identifiable ads. That doesn't take into account the types of "ads" that are subtle—such as a product strategically positioned in the hand of the movie's hero. Or the name brand shirt the pretty girl is wearing. Some experts estimate that by the time our kids are adults they will have been bombarded by literally millions of these types of ads—ads that are actually more effective in manipulating today's media-savvy teenagers.

Let me state up front: There's nothing wrong with advertising, per se. I'm a capitalist, and it is healthy competition, the "spreading of the word," the "telling the story," the "letting people know" about products and services that has helped the United States become an economic giant in the world. What parents must be aware of is that our children are not just being marketed to more forcefully and cleverly than any other generation but are often being sold a "bill of goods" about a lifestyle that will only bring them harm.

Helping children recognize deceptive advertising and understand how others try to manipulate everything from the clothes they wear to the attitude they develop to their behavior is one of the greatest services we can provide as parents. If we teach them how *not* to be manipulated as children, they will stand a better chance as adults of determining their own identities, defining their own tastes, and setting their own standards—and you just might also help them avoid the financial doldrums of debt.

SELLING SOMETHING OTHER THAN A BETTER MOUSETRAP

Today's marketers aren't targeting our kids because they want to sell them a better mousetrap; they're targeting our teens because they want to lure them *into* a trap.

In order for you to be successful at protecting your kids in today's media-saturated culture, you must never, ever underestimate the power of the forces arrayed against you. An episode of the PBS program *Frontline* entitled "The Merchants of Cool" spells out the lengths to which some marketers will and do go to manipulate our children into buying their products. It notes how today's teens are the most marketed-to group of kids in human history. This amazing documentary should be required viewing for any parent who believes that MTV is just plain ol' entertainment for today's kids.

As Douglas Rushkoff, the host of "Merchants of Cool," says, the way to get money from today's teens is to create programming that "grabs them below the belt and reaches for their wallet." Crude humor, rebellion, and sexuality are front-and-center themes in the fierce battle for our teens' wallets. Five companies—News Corp, Disney, Viacom, Universal Vivendi, and Time-Warner—fight continuously for the space in teens' brains, the one hundred fifty billion dollars they spend out of their own pockets every year, and the fifty billion more they get their parents to spend on them.

Most parents think networks, radio, and film companies are just independent businesses. Nothing could be further from the truth. Ever wonder how the content of movies, the clothes, the themes, television programs, the "look" of teen stars, and other factors can be so similar across all forms of media? It's simple: These five companies control all the major film studios, all the TV networks, most of the stations in the top TV markets, much of the radio we hear, and all or part of every major cable network.

The master at feeding crass images of sexuality and rebellion to our children is Viacom. If the name of this media giant sounds familiar, it's because they are the same folks who brought ninety million Americans Janet "Flashing" Jackson during Super Bowl 2004. While CBS whined that it had no idea that MTV was going to produce a show that included what amounted to a strip-tease act, the execs of the parent company of both broadcast outlets, Viacom, were laughing all the way to the bank.

An example of how Viacom and the others can saturate the market with their "talent" is the amazing success of their former employee, notorious sewer-mouth, Howard Stern. The autobiographical book and movie about the New York radio trash-talker was a bonanza for Viacom, which owns the publishing company Simon and Schuster. Before leaving Infinity to join the world of satellite radio, Stern's daily radio show was syndicated on some fifty stations owned by Infinity Broadcasting, a subsidiary of Viacom. Paramount Pictures, another Viacom company, made his book into a movie, and, after its successful run in theaters, the movie was distributed through Blockbuster Video, still another Viacom entity. Now you know how a foul guy like Stern can be everywhere at once.

When it comes to creating programming for teens, "Merchants of Cool" reminds us that the research conducted to control today's youth is not called "human research" or even "teen research." It's called "market research." MTV executives claim they are experts at embedding advertising into their programming so that teens don't even realize they are being bombarded with messages aimed at influencing their behavior. This confession is sobering when you take into account the following quote from "Impact of the Media on Adolescent Sexual Attitudes and Behaviors," a study by researchers at The Medical Institute in Austin, Texas:

> Data suggests that messages embedded in other media types are more powerful than direct advertising appeals

when it comes to influencing behavior. Advertising is influential, but perhaps because of how marketing-savvy teens have become, they tend to resist direct appeals to change their behaviors and are more persuaded by subtle, embedded messages. The result has been greater use of non-traditional marketing approaches, such as "viral" marketing (any strategy that encourages individuals to pass on a marketing message to others), using "trend setters" as communications sources, and e-mail. Such nontraditional sources de-emphasize the advertising aspect and highlight content to minimize the consumer's sense of being manipulated.

It's easy to see how MTV controls much of the culture in which America's teens now live. MTV is the most popular network among today's teenage girls, and the fourth most popular with boys. So many of today's girls are getting their direction for life and fashion and values through MTV. And two studies on the content of music videos and media influences on sexuality revealed that up to one-half of music videos "portray sexuality or eroticism." A 2004 report by The Medical Institute in Austin, Texas, says, "Several studies analyzing content of music videos showed that sexual intimacy was shown in over 60–75 percent of them, there was an emphasis on sexual contact without commitment, physical contact occurred at twice the rate it did on conventional television, and 81 percent of videos that showed violence also showed sexual imagery."

Can it be healthy for your daughter and her future to be on a steady diet of such programming? Admit it: your gut says, "NO!" In case you're having doubts about what your inner voice is telling you, the report also revealed that "greater music video exposure was associated with attitudes toward sexual permissiveness, higher estimates of sexual behavior among others, and more permissive attitudes toward premarital sex. In addition, teens who had preferences for watching MTV had increased levels of sexual experience."

Now are you willing to listen to your instincts?

MOOKS AND MIDRIFFS

MTV specializes in getting inside the heads of today's youth. The network is now famous in the media industry for its numerous focus groups, constant grilling of teens about their interests, intense study of today's youth—including visits by MTV executives to the homes of typical teen viewers—and the "culture spies" it dispatches to see how successfully they are impacting their target audience. All of this is done, not to figure out what teens want, but how they *think*. This most insidious use of marketing doesn't seek to satisfy the needs and desires of a mature customer; it seeks to manipulate young, impressionable minds and influence their values and lifestyle in order to sell them as much as possible.

One result of the MTV market research is the creation of female and male characters or stereotypes that are now seen in various forms in much of Viacom's empire. The male image is known as a "Mook" to industry execs, and the female is referred to as a "Midriff."

Mooks are caricatures of modern teen boys. Sort of. They are models for them to aspire to. Sort of. They are wilder and bolder and ruder and cruder than the average teen boy, but they are designed to keep our sons hyper and addicted to watching the aberrant behavior so that ever more ads can be pushed their way. They are the obnoxious pro wrestlers, the death-defying stars of the *Jackass* TV show, and the guys on MTV's Spring Break specials belching and dancing crazily with scantily clad women they met ten minutes earlier.

They exemplify perpetual adolescence living on the edge. They seem to say: "We get away with it—do what we do, look as we look—and you can, too."

"Midriff" is the name given to the female icon created by MTV. The hyper-sexualized bad girl Britney Spears and dozens of other Britney look-alikes that dominate the airwaves personify the character. The "role-model" teaches even preteen girls that it's time they embrace their sexuality and learn how to use it to their advantage; the message is that girls are sexual objects and that their sexuality is their power. That's partly why America's little girls are now bearing their bellies and strutting an attitude in malls and in schools around the country. The other reason is that parents have failed to protect their kids from becoming the victims of these clever marketing campaigns.

Not worried about the teen years yet because your kids are still toddlers? Perhaps you'll want to consider the point one reader of my column, Lisa, made in a recent e-mail:

> I have a six-year-old and a preteen in addition to my teen. Viacom does its duty on Nickelodeon and all the spin-offs from that channel. My younger girls are seeing the same images as the teens, just in a more subtle, little-girl way. Marketing is definitely targeting those age groups, preparing

them well for what lies ahead. We don't even watch MTV, but it is infiltrated through Nick so it's as if we do! What a battle we have to fight for our children's minds.

This concerned mother's e-mail gives me an opportunity to bring up two important points. The first is that media companies who want your child to like their programming at, say, fourteen, start trying to captivate them at age four. The idea is to get the kids and the parents gradually numb to certain ideas that would normally offend their sensibilities—and they start, oh, so subtly and cleverly to do so.

The second teaching lesson from this e-mail is simple: Lisa (who I believe is a well-meaning mother) recognizes the tactics of the programmers, feels uncomfortable and upset by them, yet still allows her little girls to keep watching. Unfortunately, Lisa is not an atypical parent in today's powerful pop culture.

THE "LOWER COMMON DENOMINATOR STUFF"

Does anyone actually think it's a good idea to let his or her ten-year-old daughter wear a thong or dress like a streetwalker? Yet, companies that seek to stay "on the edge" in order to make a few more bucks than their competition not only market thongs to young girls, they actually pride themselves in the action. Take the notorious clothing company, Abercrombie and Fitch. They recently got in a lot of hot water with consumers with their line of thongs designed for ten-year-olds. The thongs included the words "kiss me" and "wink, wink" and images of candy hearts and cherries.

According to a company spokesman, "It's not appropriate for a seven-year-old, but it is appropriate for a ten-year-old."

Huh?

Of course, selling sexuality to young children is nothing new for these cultural terrorists. Abercrombie and Fitch are infamous for their clothing catalogs that have featured everything from 120 pages of nudity—both top and bottom—of young girls and guys, to advocating orgies and group masturbation. A recent edition of the company's "Christmas Field Guide" said, "There are no sexual boundaries and no consequences to any sexual behavior." Yes, this is the very same company that rents prominent floor space in your local mall and sells clothes for kids as young as seven. Needless to say, my family refuses to support such propaganda with our shopping dollars.

Steven Addis, an executive with the Berkeley brand-strategy and design firm, Addis Group, explained the logic of selling the pornographic thongs to *San Francisco Chronicle* writer, Ray Delgado. Describing it as an attempt to cash in on the edgy image they've earned because of their catalogues, he said, "It's really lower common denominator stuff when you have to resort to this kind of surreptitious type of product to get people into the store."

Addis is right on both counts: it is "lower common denominator," and it does bring folks into the store.

So here's a question: how many ten-year-olds drive themselves to the mall, find their way to the store, plunk down the cash, and then make their way back home again? Answer: zero. It's parents that engage in such stupidity—even though it goes against their better judgment to do so.

I once knew a mother who told me that she was very

disappointed in herself for having purchased her eleven-year-old a thong. She had stifled that inner voice in the pit of her stomach and had, instead, given in to the pressure from her daughter and the mother of her daughter's friend to buy the "underwear."

"I'll bet you think I'm a horrible parent—gosh, I feel so bad, but I just didn't know how to say no." "I don't think you're a horrible parent," I responded. "I just don't understand why you are giving the culture and another mother so much power over your decisions regarding your own daughter." "You're right," the mom responded. "I copped out. I should be stronger."

This otherwise wonderful mother had made a dreadful mistake. Although she thought the issue was merely about the thong, the real issue is how she—as the mother and role model for her daughter—had never learned to exercise good judgment and stand up to peer pressure. If a forty-something woman can't stand up to peer pressure when buying undergarments, for pity's sake, how on earth can she expect her daughter to take a stand as she goes through the tumultuous teen years? She also obviously had allowed her daughter to consume media that pumped her with the idea that wearing a thong was something to be desired. Go figure.

If you've fallen into the trap of letting Susie or Johnnie go to their room to watch MTV for hours on end because you don't want to be bothered, or because "other moms let their kids do it," or because you haven't taken the time to actually sit down and view the programming for yourself, it's high time you find out what's going on and consider setting your kids free from the machine that is using them.

Moms, Dads, listen to that inner voice. When your first reaction to the cultural fad of the day—whether it is MTV programming or the purchase of a clothing item made popular by crafty marketers—is disgust or even doubt about its appropriateness for your child, I encourage you to act on your inner voice. I'm not asking you to let my standards become yours, I'm encouraging you to investigate, think about what you are teaching your kids, and then follow your instincts instead of giving into outside pressures that have no real concern or interest in your child (except for the financial exploitation of them).

A good place to start is by ordering "The Merchants of Cool" from PBS.org and watching it by yourself. If your kids are older teens, you may then wish to watch it with them. Showing them exactly how they are being manipulated is a powerful tool. A final warning: you may be shocked by some of the images in "Merchants," but if your kids watch MTV, they won't be. Things have really gotten that bad.

SELLING SELFISHNESS TO CHILDREN

So just what does McDonald's put on those Big Macs?

Let's hear it, everyone thirty or older. A one, and a two, and a . . . "Two all-beef patties, special sauce, lettuce, cheese, pickles, onions on a sesame-seed bun."

We also know things go better with Coke, Gillette is the best a man can get, and Domino's delivers.

We know because we've heard these themes thousands of times in commercials. We learn a lot from advertisers, and we seem to remember it forever.

This is no accident, of course. Advertising companies spend billions of dollars to determine precisely how to reach each demographic they have determined is "their market." And over the last twenty years, children make up more of those audiences, and companies have learned how to capitalize on it.

This may not seem so bad when it's, say, McDonald's and Wendy's competing for a kid's dollar-hamburger. But think about some of the slogans kids encounter: "Why wait?" "Obey your thirst." "No boundaries." "Got the urge?" In other words, be selfish, instantly gratify yourself, regardless of the consequences. And remember, "He who dies with the most toys wins."

It's important to understand that a key element of today's advertising strategy is to create discontent in the hearts and minds of all of us. My husband and I took a family financial course, and in the workbook there was a powerful illustration of how effective the marketing of "discontentment" can be. The authors of the Crown Financial Ministries materials told the story of an "American company that opened a new plant in Central America because the labor there was relatively inexpensive. Everything went well until the villagers received their first paycheck; afterward they did not return to work. Several days later, the manager went down to the village chief to determine the cause of this problem, and the chief responded, 'Why should we work? We already have everything we need.' The plant stood idle for two months until someone came up with the idea of sending a mail-order catalog to every villager. There has not been an employment problem since!"

It's a powerful example of how discontentment makes money. Although all it took in a simple country was a catalog to get otherwise contented people to spend their money, in a culture as complicated and chaotic as ours, marketers have a much tougher job. Our kids are bombarded with so many voices trying to get their attention that the only way a marketer can reach them is to play on their emotions. Teens are especially vulnerable to this age-old marketing trick because, as every parent of a teenager knows, teens' emotions are, shall we say, all over the place.

Part of growing up is wanting to be independent—to stretch your wings. Add a dose of discontentment and sprinkle on a little disrespect to that natural, healthy drive for independence, and you end up with an extremely explosive attitude known as rebellion. Cast your products in the guise of characters who display these attitudes, and you've not only got the attention of teens, you can easily manipulate them. Teenagers are also walking hormone combustion engines. They're discovering their sexuality, and their blood can run hot with desire from only the slightest encouragement. Fill an ad campaign with scantily clad babes and studs, and Presto! You've got teens eating right out of your hand and reaching for their wallets.

Kids also thrive on the rush of adrenaline. And nothing gets adrenaline pumping more than rage. Add rebellion and sex to rage, create a beat to go with it, and you've got gangsta rap. This particular form of "entertainment" was created specifically to play on the explosive emotions of children who already have a tendency to feel left out or abandoned. It is particularly popular in communities where fathers are scarce, and violence and drug abuse are rampant. By speaking in a language to which this group can relate, the genre has gained a loyal following whose naïve fans don't even realize that the stars are feeding their hostility and discontent simply to make millions. The kids from broken homes who thrive on this "music" are being used by an industry composed of people who have no regard that they are actually making these kids' lives worse. And, like any form of media entertainment, when gangsta rap started bringing in the bucks, it went mainstream. How many bucks? More than $1.5 billion in 2003.

And what do the children who buy these records get to hear? Here are a few quick, edited samples:

"Hoe, you gotta go if you ain't takin' off ya clothes
All I really wanna do is stick a d—k up in you."
　　　　　　—"Tha Dogg Pound Feat" by Crooked I

"F—k AmeriKKKa, still with the triple K
'Cause you know when my nine goes buck
It'll bust your head like a watermelon dropped from twelve stories up."
　　　　　　—"The Wrong Nigga To F—k With" by Ice Cube

"Pray that she abort that, if she's talking about keepin' it.
One hit to the stomach, she's leakin' it."
—Joe Budden's remix of the hit song "Confessions, Part II"

I'm going to go out on a limb and guess that you'd rather *not* have your children listen to such highbrow material.

IT ALL BEGINS AT HOME

If these are not the messages you want your child to hear and/or act on—and surveys show that overwhelming majorities of parents fall into this category—it's up to you to do something about it. One step might be to join forces with the Motherhood Project, an operation of the Institute for American Values. The project has brought together moms from all walks of life and political persuasions that, according to an open letter from the moms to advertisers, have declared themselves "in rebellion against a popular culture that is waging war on our children."

The Motherhood Project is long on benefit of the doubt, but short on patience with advertisers. "We do not believe that you intend to harm our children," the letter states. "Perhaps you don't recognize that you are harming them. But you are harming them with such growing intensity, and with such grave consequences for their well-being, that we have no choice but to challenge you directly as a vital step in reversing the tide that has turned against our children."

But they want advertisers to take the letter's contents to heart. They want to see more Chick-Fil-A's out there—companies that position themselves (truthfully) as family-friendly. They want advertisers to cross over to their side in the culture wars with cleaner commercials and more appropriate products. They want executives to truly consider whether it's a good idea to, say, sell clothes that make young girls look like streetwalkers-in-training.

These parents (the Project welcomes dads and grandparents, too) are ready to talk with companies that want to do better and to extend all manner of understanding to those trying to improve. And they are more than willing to walk away from those that don't take them seriously.

And let's not forget, folks: values education begins at home.

Many of us need to take a look inward and commit to improve-
ment—to lead less media-driven, work-driven, and consump-
tion-driven lives. We need to work harder to assert our values and
ourselves into the lives of our children. We need to teach them to
deconstruct the messages advertisers send. We may not desire to
make our homes and families commerce-free, but that doesn't
mean we can't work to minimize advertising's influence. And
there is no reason for our children to be bombarded by advertising, marketing, or market research in their schools. None. And we
should see that they don't.

We should join the Motherhood Project in urging advertisers
to quit targeting the youngest of children with messages of selfishness and instant gratification and to stop sponsoring sexually
graphic or violent programming created for kids.

We hope, of course, advertisers will work with parents on the
all-important and terribly difficult job of watching out for our
kids. But if they won't, we need to show them we mean business.
We need to show them who really controls the money in the family. And it's not the eight-year-old.

4

FOUNDATION OF FAITH

The small child froze in her footsteps and slightly cocked her head to listen more carefully. *What was that sound?*

In the stillness of the hallway near the family bedrooms, she heard it again. It sounded like a low, mournful cry . . . a soulful weeping.

Knowing that her daddy was the only other person home, she tiptoed silently and slowly toward his room, filled with concern and curiosity. As she drew closer, the little girl could see that the door stood slightly ajar. She gently pushed it open just enough to peer inside.

A sense of holiness permeated the air, and, in an instant, her impressionable young mind and spirit were impacted so deeply that she would embrace the memory of that moment countless times throughout her life.

I was that little girl, and what I experienced that day some thirty years ago would forever define my father and guide my faith.

In the solace of his room, I saw my daddy kneeling beside his bed weeping and praying from the depths of his soul for one of his young patients. As the tears flowed freely from this great man,

I lingered for a moment in breathless awe as I felt my faith in God soar beyond my own understanding.

My Papa Doc, as he affectionately became known in his later years, was a Johns Hopkins-educated pediatrician. He was the epitome of the brilliant, loving physician often portrayed in Norman Rockwell paintings. His commitment to his young patients was all-encompassing, with the end of a long day's work often finding him immersed in medical journals so that he might remain on the cutting edge of treatment advances.

Much more than a practitioner and student of medicine, my dad was a man of God. And on that day many years ago as I peeked into his room to discover the source of the mystical sound, it became clear that my daddy relied on the awesome power and wisdom of the Great Physician to guide him.

Although my father died in 2002, his faith continues to impact my life.

Dad lavished love and comfort on tens of thousands of children over a career that spanned nearly forty-five years. Had he not been limited by age and illness, Dad would have chosen to care for and serve his patients until his last breath. His immense compassion for the hurting and the lonely was a reflection of the Christ who lived in him.

Humble in spirit, yet confident in the Word of God, Dad didn't just "practice" his faith—he lived it. He studied diligently, worked tirelessly, and prayed endlessly. He was a quiet man, but his actions boldly proclaimed the hope and grace that came as a result of his undying faith.

Dad loved, trusted, and adored my mother in a manner rarely found in marriages today. His actions and heart toward Mom exemplified a biblical command that many don't even know exists: "Husbands, love your wives as Christ loved the Church, and even gave himself up for her."

He was a man of honor and the quintessential Southern gentleman. He approached others with the greatest of respect, defended those unjustly treated, and kept silent when personally offended.

For Dad, honesty wasn't the best policy; it was the only policy. I recall driving by a beautiful Georgia cotton field during a family vacation one summer. Having never seen a "snow-topped" crop before, my brothers and sister and I started begging Mom and Dad to stop so we could pick a few. Dad explained that it wouldn't be right to take even one of what didn't belong to us. We then proceeded to drive for several miles well out of our way in search of the farmer's house to ask permission. The farmer graciously gave us some cotton, but the real gift that day came from our dad.

Ever mindful of his own shortcomings and imperfections, Dad privately called on the mercy, wisdom, and grace of God throughout each day. If you looked closely, oftentimes you could see his lips moving ever so slightly in prayer as he worked, walked, or read.

Dr. Henry J. Redd Jr. lived the life we should all strive for. He wasn't just a good man; he was extraordinary. I count it among the greatest of blessings to be his daughter.

WHAT IS MY LEGACY?

Throughout my seventeen years of motherhood, I have often thought about the impact of those few seconds of watching Dad in prayer. It makes me wonder . . . what are the snapshots of my motherhood that will most impact the lives of my own children?

What are the lessons of faith, of morality, of *living* that I am teaching my kids through my actions? It's a sobering thought—but one every parent must ponder. My father never even knew I had been watching him pray. Yet, his private act of faith—meshed with how he lived his life on a daily basis—became the cornerstone for the development of how I should live my life as a whole person.

Many people mistakenly believe they can separate their various roles in life. One moment they are mother, the next, wife, then they are daughter, who is not to be confused with the independent woman. To view one's life as so segmented is to forget a basic fundamental reality: Each of us has one soul. And although we may—and should—relate quite differently as a mother to our children than we do as a professional with our colleagues, or a wife to her husband, the message of our hearts must be the same in every circumstance. Our faith is the unifying theme that pulls together and makes sense of all the various roles we have in our lives. If our behavior and beliefs are consistently marked by love and commitment to timeless values—no matter the circumstances, no matter who the other characters are—we can then be at peace and live the life that will naturally serve as an example that our own children will want to follow.

When you carefully review the story about my father, it is obvious that the thread that wove all the roles and stories of his life into one incredibly inspirational tapestry was his commitment to his Christian beliefs. He not only practiced his faith in private, he practiced it as a well-educated professional doctor; he practiced it as a father on vacation with his family; he practiced it in his marriage; he practiced it in his community. In short, it was his faith—put into action in all aspects of his life—that defined the man, rather than the various roles.

Oh, don't get me wrong—Dad wasn't perfect. But in the midst of the personal struggles with his own weaknesses, again, it was his faith that helped him through. His faith wasn't a *part* of his life—it *was* his life. His faith was intricately woven throughout every scene; it was the very lifeblood that fed everything he did.

It is essential that you stop and ask yourself a few basic questions: What is it that I believe? In whom do I put my trust? What values are so important that I will commit to naturally incorporating them into every aspect of my life? In short, how do I define my faith?

If you don't find answers to these questions, you will never be able to successfully teach your children how to define their own faith. If your personal values are wavering, or if they are dependent on the latest fad, or a shifting definition of morality—you will not be able to live at peace with yourself over decisions regarding your children or have any real chance of teaching them how to be at peace in our chaotic culture.

Your children *want* to learn about faith and spirituality, and if you don't inspire them to fill that void in their souls with God, their creator and guardian, someone will likely help them fill it with something else.

An article by Associated Press reporter Rachel Zoll put parents on notice in September of 2004 that even *Seventeen* magazine—noted for its articles on sex and fashion—is getting into the faith business. Zoll reported that the magazine has a new "faith section that includes inspirational messages, personal stories of spiritual struggle, and testimonials on issues that include prayer and gay teenagers who attend church." Zoll summarizes one column, "Faiza worships five times a day, while Rhianna is as likely to believe in the Easter Bunny as in God. Kristin prays, too, but to the God and the Goddess."

The editor of the magazine, Atoosa Rubenstein, told Zoll that she wants to give girls a place to discuss faith and religion, which she believes this generation of girls finds important. "I just noticed, more and more, our readers were talking about their faith."

Zoll went on to say, "Experts on religion and youth trends agree. They theorize that teenagers are rebelling against the broad, undefined spirituality of their baby-boomer parents and are seeking out environments—like those in church—with clearer rules that help them cope with day-to-day problems."

Parents, this report is a *gift* of information to you about your kids. They *want* you to set rules for them. They *want* to know what is right and what is wrong. They *want* you to teach them about God and faith and His undying love for them. And if you don't, your children will learn about spirituality from somewhere else, and it may do them more harm than good.

I recently became acquainted with a mother of two daughters who had suffered through a painful divorce several years ago. The resulting trauma for the girls, compounded by the fact that neither parent talked much about faith, sent the girls searching for something to give their lives meaning. They ended up in a Goth group that, as their mom put it, is "obsessed with vampires." The girls are accomplished equestrians, from a wealthy family, go to one of the best academic schools in the nation, *and are heavily into witchcraft*.

Think it can't happen to your children? Neither did this mother. We are all spiritual beings in need of something greater than ourselves. That need will either be filled with truth or filled with a lie, but it will be filled.

But please understand that the primary reason to examine your faith is not because your children require it of you; you must define your faith because it is the right thing to do for yourself. Let me say that again, you must define your faith because it is the right thing to do for *yourself*. Once you have grounded yourself in faith and committed to live and uphold specific principles, the beautiful, miraculous reality is that everyone around you will benefit—*especially* your family and children.

FAITH FOR TODAY FROM TIMES PAST

In addition to my father's influence on my life in helping me determine "In whom do I believe?" and "In what do I place my trust?" my mother was also a guiding light for me—especially through the normally tumultuous teen years. But I've decided to wait and share those examples with you in Chapter Nine. To illustrate how bedrock values of faith are timeless, I'd like to share an example now of my grandmother's influence on all those around her.

In my grandmother's last days, her once fluffy, dark brown hair had become silky and white as fresh snow; her once supple skin had become as thin and delicate as translucent tissue paper stretched over bony fingers; and her formerly piercing jet-black eyes could only blankly stare at her surroundings.

She knew nothing of the terror that enveloped a nation on that fateful day now known as 9/11, nothing of the panic that struck at the hearts of millions of U.S. citizens, nothing of the evil murderous thug named bin Laden. When my grandmother died on September 26, 2001, death came silently and mercifully.

Muggie, as we called her, was ninety-four years old. She lived through two World Wars, the Great Depression, the civil unrest of the '60s, and the media revolution. She was the last of twelve siblings to leave this world, and as she took her final breath, an era came to an end.

Muggie's generation witnessed countless inventions, the rise and fall of Communism in the former Soviet Union, and the dawning of the computer age. She left us at a time when Americans discovered that the brutality of modern warfare would no longer just be "over there," but would be painfully wrought in our own cities, on our own soil. Thank God, my dear Muggie didn't know that the new enemy often lives among us, awaiting the perfect time to betray our trust as he engages in a murderous, destructive rampage.

My siblings and I spent many sweltering but wonderful summer days and nights in our grandparents' home in Tallahassee, Florida. Muggie was of the old-school décor: crocheted doilies on the tables and sofas, the hand embroidered pillowcases, and the photographs of countless relatives I didn't know. Her house always smelled of roasting beef, stewing mustard greens, and brewing tea. When diluted, the pitcher of warm tea would be left one-quarter of the way empty so that massive amounts of sugar could be poured in. I remember stirring and stirring and stirring, watching the cloudy liquid gradually turn a caramel brown as the sugar finally dissolved. The finished product was so sweet you could almost imagine mushy rock candy crystals forming on the sides of the large squares of ice that filled the colored glasses we drank from.

Muggie grew up in South Georgia, and every summer she would take us to the "old home place" to visit her one surviving brother and several sisters. I recall happy times chasing the chickens and frantically running from the angry rooster; of peering in the dusty silo at what seemed like millions of ears of dried corn; of gleefully riding on the back of old Great-Uncle Wilsey's red tractor; of the maddening feeling of dried Georgia red clay under my fingernails and up my nose; and of struggling to cuddle the cute but wild kittens that hung around the house, only to have my arms and hands severely scratched—yet again. I remember the visits with Great-Aunt Melissa and the delight of savoring every bite of her deliciously sweet homemade divinity as we sat in her parlor and visited with kind but somewhat curious great aunts and distant cousins.

Back at Muggie's house, I looked forward to the visits with my dad's only brother, Uncle Bryan Lee. He always had a twinkle in his eye and a humorous story to tell about his and my father's childhood. I treasured these visits with my uncle—he was the bridge between the loving but strict demeanor of my grandparents and my own carefree, happy childhood dreams. His stories and rascal-like humor made my grandparents seem more human. And although it was evident he did not embrace all of their formal ways and rules, he always—always—treated them with respect. It was Uncle Bryan Lee that kept a watchful eye on my Muggie in the thirty years she spent as a widow. It was this fun-loving uncle of mine and his wife, Aunt Sally, who nurtured and lovingly cared for my precious grandmother when her body and mind began to betray her with age.

My most vivid childhood memories of time spent with Granddaddy Redd and Muggie were the nightly Bible readings and lengthy prayers spent on our knees in the front room. These sessions before bed were both welcomed and dreaded rituals for squirming children. My grandfather would reverently, emotionally lead these sessions of thanksgiving and petition to a God that was very real. Granddaddy and Muggie were often moved to tears, their authoritative manner temporarily shed as they openly bared their hearts before God and the grandchildren that knelt around them. As a very young child, I sometimes drifted in and out of sleep as they earnestly prayed for old folks I didn't know. But sometimes I would cry with them, deeply moved both by their compassion for others and by their undying faith in God and His mercy, even while they prayed about suffering they could not understand.

It is this faith that I now cling to. When I think of the injustice and devastation and human suffering levied on thousands of innocent civilians on 9/11; when I witness how our nation was severely crippled by unspeakable evil; when I see the selfishness and pressures of a culture that would have my children throw virtue to the wind; when I look into their eyes and fear for their future; I often return in my mind's eye to the front room of my grandparents' home and remember their absolute trust in the God of all creation. I feel free to weep before Him and mourn the losses and suffering I do not understand. I recall that the values of purity, of integrity, of honesty, and of the courage to set oneself apart from the culture are just as important today as they were then. And just as Granddaddy and Muggie wiped their tears and rose to their feet with renewed strength at the end of their prayers, I do the same. The lessons I learned from my grandparents were lessons of faith and triumph. And the source of both is still the same: a loving God who is always just a prayer away.

FINDING TIME FOR FEEDING FAITH

But why does it often seem so very difficult to find the time to talk with God?

Life is busy: the phone keeps ringing, the kids need my attention. Meanwhile, someone's at the door, the dog is barking, there are bills to be paid, I have a deadline at work . . . but where is the time for God?

He doesn't pound on the door like the neighborhood children, or stand beside my desk and interrupt while I'm working, or call during dinner like the phone solicitors.

No, He patiently waits for *me* to call on *Him*.

While the stresses are building, and I try to figure out schedules, or why we're already out of milk (again), and who's picking up whom from what, *God waits*.

While I throw another load of laundry in the washer, direct my child to sweep the kitchen floor, sort through the mail and answer another phone call, *God waits*.

My husband and I find time each day for a private conversation over a cup of coffee. We take the time to show love toward our children and discuss their schoolwork and their concerns. Their friends frequently spend the night, and we even manage to fix homemade donuts for the entire gang. Meanwhile, *God waits*.

The period from September of 2001 through September of 2002 was a horrendous time for me. First, the nation was shaken from terrorist attacks. Within two short weeks, my personal world began shaking from a series of deaths, beginning with dear Muggie. At the same time, my mother was dying of painful, lingering bone cancer. In the midst of her suffering, the love of her life and her primary caretaker—my sweet daddy—dropped dead of a heart attack. Three weeks later, one of my best friends died. I had three emergency-room visits for various injuries with my children in less than five weeks. My mother, lonely and heartbroken, was finally overpowered by the evil of cancer and slipped away just one month later. A previous back injury of mine was aggravated from the physical care I gave my mom in her dying hours, resulting in the rupture of two of my lower discs and landing me in tremendous pain and in bed for days on end. Unlike any other time in my life, I was struck by the brevity and fragility of life and found myself reflective and quiet—and waiting for God to change my world.

I believe in miracles. I don't think it was an accident that during that most difficult period of my life I met Shirley Dobson and heard about her book, *Certain Peace in Uncertain Times*. It's no coincidence that at the very time in my life when I most needed help, the Father of mercy and love brought me a book to teach me how to pray, written by a woman who understood and had lived through many challenges—and who had emerged triumphant, with her faith and values intact.

I remember sitting in my sunroom on a bright morning, reading the words of a woman whose heart's desire is to share the joy of prayer. I wept and my own heart ached as I rediscovered just how much God wants to hear from *me*.

Why—again I ask—does it often seem so very difficult to find the time to talk to God? We know from personal experience that prayer is effective, and powerful and healing. It has the ability to change us, to strengthen us, to give us peace. Yet, it is often the very last thing we take the time to do—often finding ourselves falling into bed, exhausted, and whispering a few words as we drift off to sleep.

As I was pondering these questions in the back of my mind, I came across a section in Shirley Dobson's book that grabbed my attention: "Yet God does not abandon us. He keeps His promise: 'Never will I leave you; never will I forsake you.' (Hebrews 13:5). Even during the storms, He stands just to the side, ever watchful, waiting to embrace us the moment we again seek His presence. His words to Jeremiah apply to us all: 'Call to me and I will answer you.' (Jeremiah 33:3)."

I paused, breathless, and read the verse again: "*Call to me and I will answer you.*" I was numb as I tried to absorb the thought that the God of all Creation has commanded me to call on Him. My mind couldn't then—and still can't—begin to comprehend the fact that He then promises to answer *me*.

As I scanned through her book, Shirley's message became quite clear: God desires to have deep, personal, frequent conversations with me. With me? *With me!*

I became a Christian during Sunday school class when I was about five years old. It was a very personal, very real moment of transformation. I knew beyond any shadow of a doubt that the God of Creation had taken me in His arms and become my Lord. All it took, on my part, was a simple prayer of faith.

Throughout my life I have called on God, searching for wisdom, or seeking comfort, or simply exclaiming joyous praise. I have felt the power of prayer many times and seen how effective it is.

Yet, I am ashamed to admit, I have also often neglected to talk to God. Sometimes I was too tired, sometimes I was too busy. Maybe even sometimes I was just too selfish.

But, thanks to the examples of my parents and grandparents, and thanks to books like Shirley Dobson's, I'm always brought back to the reality that prayer is an essential part of being all that I can be, of being a better mother—and a better person.

It's so awesome to know I don't have to go it alone.

And you don't have to either.

Whether you are happily married, or going through a painful time in your marriage, or raising children as a single parent, you are not alone.

Weathering life's struggles and raising kids in a culture that has gone mad takes strength and guidance from someone bigger, wiser, and stronger than ourselves. And He's always only a prayer away.

FAITH IN ACTION

The first step in protecting your family from a culture that's stark raving mad is to figure out your values and faith, and that includes living them. This is the foundation on which every tactical suggestion, every effort to instill strong character, every step taken to protect your family, must be based.

If your faith and actions are weak, or in question, or are inconsistent, you will lose the battle personally, and will leave your children helpless, destined to wander through a killer culture without a compass and with no weapons of protection.

Children (teens included) are looking for limits, searching for guidance, and hoping for something firm to believe in. Only if you have answered these questions yourself will you be able to help them succeed. And it is only when you earn their respect that your words will have meaning. Of this you can be certain: kids can spot a phony in a flash, and when they do, the phony becomes the object of their scorn.

It has been said that "he who believes in everything, believes in nothing." How true. Honesty, integrity, purity, honor, kindness, courage, goodness, joy, peace, patience, faithfulness, gentleness, and self-control are all under attack from today's culture. Yet, these are the virtues that every parent wants to see reflected in their child. But unless we clearly teach our children that we believe in these values, and show them that we live them, our kids will be in danger of falling victim to the siren song of cheap imitations marketed through empty promises of fulfillment.

Our challenge and responsibilities as parents are mind-boggling, to say the least. But with a firm faith in God, a commitment to walking the walk, and with a daily dose of prayer and reinforcement, we can raise children who will be victors and champions of character and life.

In your family, it all starts with you.

5

MOMS AND DADS
LOVING EACH OTHER

If we're going to fight the toxic culture—and after you're done reading this book, I believe you'll be inspired to do just that—we have to make certain that we go about it the right way. As you can probably guess, it's going to involve a lot of vigilance and courage on your part. It's going to mean keeping a sharp eye out for the most pernicious influences and taking stands that may not be very popular, either with your children or with other parents who are less conscientious.

In addition to establishing your faith, there's something else you have to do first if you're to succeed in raising children who are grounded, courageous, and fulfilled. It's one of the most important things you can do because it provides a steady force, a place of comfort for your children in a harsh world, and more joy *for you* than you could ever imagine: love your spouse.

Sounds simple, doesn't it? After all, few of us would have gotten married if we didn't love that one someone, right? Yet virtually all of us have experienced marital problems in some form or another—some much more severe than others. And we don't need piles of scientific research (although there's plenty out there) to know the harmful effects that marital problems have on couples and on their children. Naturally, our efforts to fight a toxic culture will be compromised, to say the least, when children suffer the misfortune of a broken home.

This is not to say that every couple that has endured a breakup or a separation of some kind—or perhaps is together but fighting constantly—is comprised of bad people. But whatever the cause of the strife, it's no use pretending that our children aren't affected, often profoundly so. Spouses who have gone through a divorce seldom have the energy or the creativity needed to fight the culture effectively. In fact, they sometimes compete with their former spouses, trying to be the "cool parent," the one who lets the children go where they please and spend time with whomever they like, as if good parenting consisted of winning a popularity contest.

Most couples considering marriage very much want their marriage to succeed, but this desire can lead many of them to make a profound mistake. I'm talking about the so-called "trial marriage," or what our grandmothers bluntly called "shacking up." Recent figures show that more than half of all couples that plan to get married live together first. Does this step help them avoid divorce court? You may be surprised to learn that the truth is quite the opposite: it dramatically increases the chances of divorce later on.

The numbers are in: a 2004 book entitled, *The Family Portrait*, by the Family Research Council (which can be downloaded for a donation at FRC.org) reveals that couples who cohabit before marriage are 46 percent more likely to divorce once they do get married than couples who don't live together first. The statistics compiled by FRC also show that cohabitators suffer from more depression, alcoholism, poorer relationships with other family members and experience less happiness in general than do married couples.

Surprised? You shouldn't be. Psychologically speaking, what are we saying when we decide to go the trial-marriage route? "You know, I'm not so sure things will work out with you. I'd better test things out first." Whether we mean to or not, we're sending a message that our own safety comes before our trust in the person we supposedly love.

More important, though, the bedrock principle of a man and woman having sex and living together only within the commitment of marriage was clearly stated long ago by a loving God who knew it would be for the benefit of us and our children.

For those who are quick to dismiss FRC's statistics as religious propaganda, you should know that the organization neither conducted nor commissioned the studies that reveal what most people instinctively know, but consistently ignore: a stable family unit is the foundation for a stable society and for raising stable children.

The Family Portrait is a "compilation of data, social research, and polling on contemporary American attitudes regarding marriage and family." The book includes both current data as well as historical trends on a variety of issues including marriage, childcare, unwed childbearing, divorce, and cohabitation. Each fact is carefully documented and footnoted with the name of the research organization, medical facility, agency, or polling company responsible for the particular statistic. Scores of various sources are referenced, providing the most comprehensive data ever compiled on issues of concern to the family.

And the verdict is overwhelming. As Ken Connor, the former president of FRC put it, "The crisis in marriage and family is real, and its implications for America's future are chilling. No civilization can long endure without strong, healthy families founded on the inviolable institution of marriage as the lifelong union of one man and one woman." And, I would add, no fight against the culture can long endure without a marriage founded on genuine selflessness and loving commitment.

Creating sound, stable families is so obviously the answer to saving our society from a litany of social ills and heartbreak—also detailed in The Heritage Foundation's "Family and Society Database," available for free at Heritage.org—that it's almost astounding in its simplicity. Yet Americans, it seems, would rather have the government throw billions and billions of dollars in continued ill attempts to fix what are, at the core, moral and personal problems than they would proclaim the truth and accept the personal responsibility necessary to be a part of the stable family units we all crave.

Government policy often endorses the broken family through handouts and endless programs and levies penalty taxes against individuals who contribute to the stability of our society through marriage. Add that to the endless barrage of Hollywood propaganda (a.k.a. entertainment) that idolizes adultery, casual sex, divorce, and homosexuality, and it's no surprise to discover that America has seen a marked decline in the number of marriages that occur each year in every age group since 1970.

Commitment. Love. Integrity. Faithfulness. These are clear virtues upon which we must stand, both as individuals and as a nation. It's time for us to reach back for the sake of the future and reclaim those timeless values upon which our families and nation will rise or fall. There are right and wrong choices. When individuals make the right choices regarding a commitment to marriage and to their families, they and society are better for it.

A short, simple e-mail I received from a reader of my weekly column provides evidence from someone who has made a career out of knowing and working with kids:

> Your article about marriage was great. I have been a youth sports coach/official for many years. One thing I notice about successful students in both academics and athletics is that they almost always have a stable home life with both a caring mother and father living together.

Still not convinced? As they say, a picture is worth a thousand words. Here are a few more snapshots from *The Family Portrait* and the Heritage family database:

- Women are safer in marriage

- Children are safer in homes with married parents

- Children in homes with married parents are healthier and engage in less risky behavior

- Children in cohabiting households are likely to have emotional and behavioral problems and experience greater educational difficulties

- Cohabiting households are more likely to be poor than are married-couple families

- Children from broken homes are more likely to engage in delinquent behavior

America must promote and encourage the inherent value in strong marriages and families if we are to survive as a nation. If we as a society continue to promote and casually accept cohabitation, rampant divorce, sex outside of marriage, and homosexual partnerships as alternatives to traditional marriage, we can expect more poverty, more crime, more emotional problems, and more social chaos.

But let's get personal for a moment. If you're one of those folks who lived with your spouse before marriage, or otherwise entered marriage with a "let's see" attitude, you don't have to be just another statistic in the nation's divorce ledger. You can start today with a fresh approach and firm commitment to your marriage. If you need a marriage counselor, get a marriage counselor. I'm constantly amazed at how much time and energy people put into to sports or hobbies and things that don't really matter in the end. Yet, they put very little time and effort into the single most important relationship of their lives. It might be tough going for a while to dig through all the emotions that have been buried for so long, but giving your marriage everything you've got, and then giving it more, is worth it in the end. There are resources in the back of this book under the heading of "Marriage" that can give you direction, support, and real help for making your marriage succeed. Please use them.

PRESERVING MARRIAGE

Clearly, there's nothing more important to a child's future than to be raised in a home with both a mom and a dad who are committed to each other. Yet, there are a few folks who want to eliminate a mother or father from the start. Yes, I'm referring to what seems to be the only context in which most of us even hear about marriage today—when we're discussing the same-sex variety.

Marriage is the legal union of one man and one woman. It's simple, yet powerful. It's so basic to who we are, so absolutely mandated by the laws of nature, that its critical place in society would seem beyond explanation. From time immemorial, the family—starting with marriage between one man and woman—has been the foundation of every civil society around the world. To alter that unit now would be to embark upon the single greatest social experiment in America's history. Matthew Spalding, Ph.D., of The Heritage Foundation's Simon Center for American Studies, points out,

> What is happening is not a slight change in degree that merely extends benefits or rights to a larger class, but a substantive change in the essence of the institution. It does not expand marriage; it alters its core meaning, for to redefine marriage so that it is not intrinsically related to the relationship between fathers, mothers, and children would sever the institution from its nature and purpose.

If the composition of marriage were changed, in just one or two generations the landscape of America would be irrevocably altered, affecting not just the family, but every other institution as well. If you weaken the foundation upon which a society is built, the result is a weaker society that will eventually crumble.

It's as elementary as the story of "The Three Little Pigs." Who doesn't understand the moral of this childhood fable? The strength of a home is determined by the materials from which the structure is built. Build the house from straw, and you've got a weaker structure than one made from brick. It's just that simple.

The same basic principle applies to a society. But instead of bricks or straw, the building element of every society is the family unit. Change the composition of the family, and you also change the look, feel, and strength of the society in which those families live.

If there are to be children, it is the man and woman who make them. Like I said, this is pretty basic stuff. When explained to children this story is often entitled, "The Birds and the Bees."

The important lessons taught in both "The Three Little Pigs" and "The Birds and the Bees" are not merely religious tenets to be discarded at will but are universal, undeniable fundamentals of life.

The old adage, "As the family goes, so goes the nation," is as undeniably true as are the facts of life. Of course, individual families undergo natural changes over the years. Death often enters the picture, causing some children to be displaced or left with one parent, or different parents altogether. But just as bricks age, with one here or there becoming weaker, the strength of the many maintains the integrity of the overall structure.

However, the significant increase in divorce and children

being born out of wedlock in recent years has caused American society to weaken and has resulted in a plethora of problems. Too many broken families, like too many broken bricks, threaten our entire society with collapse.

My Heritage colleague, researcher and policy analyst Pat Fagan, says that American children and families are living in a "culture of rejection."

In testimony Pat gave before the United States Senate committee, he explained, "When parents reject each other by divorce or an out-of-wedlock birth that eventually ends in totally separate lives for the father and mother, the strengths of their children are not as developed as they could be, and more weaknesses occur in major outcomes such as deprivations, addictions, abuse, and failure."

He went on to say, "In 1950, for every hundred children born that year, twelve entered a broken family—four were born out of wedlock and eight suffered the divorce of their parents. By the year 2000, that number had risen fivefold, and for every one hundred children born, sixty entered a broken family, with thirty-three of those born out of wedlock, and twenty-seven suffering the divorce of both parents."

He added, "We must conclude that over the last fifty years America has changed from being preponderantly 'a culture of belonging' to now being 'a culture of rejection.'"

Pat then outlined the damage of a culture marked as such:

Because of this level of the rejection by fathers and mothers of each other this growing cohort of children has not nor will not attain the fullness of its capacities. Neither can the nation attain the fullness of its capacity to fulfill its destiny and role.

The children of parents who reject each other suffer: in deep emotional pain, ill health, depression, anxiety, even shortened lifespan; more drop out of school, fewer go to college, they earn less income, they develop more addiction to drugs and alcohol, and they engage in increased violence or suffer it within their own homes.

Society also suffers with more gangs, more assaults, more violence against women and children, more sexual abuse of women and children, and much bigger bills for jails, increased need for health care, supplemental education, addiction programs, foster care, homelessness prevention programs, and on and on. The expansion of all these social program budgets is directly linked to the breakdown of marriage.

AND IT COULD GET MUCH WORSE

Those smug individuals who seek to radically overturn American society by further weakening the family structure are so clever in their tactics that many Americans are in the same position as the proverbial frog in the pot. The temperature has been turned up so gradually over the years that the poor sot doesn't know his own goose is about to be cooked. And those who would redefine the family, with the help of the mass media, are turning up the heat every day.

You would think that marriage belongs on that short list of things in America you just can't oppose, such as mom, apple pie, and jobs. Everybody knows you can't be against good schools or clean air or low crime rates. Surely marriage is beyond reproach.

Forget it. All couples that are trying to fight the culture need to know a stark reality: there are radical activists who are actively seeking to trash society's most venerable institution.

We can't let this challenge go unanswered. It's important that we help people understand that the health and structure of our nation is directly linked to the health and structure of our marriages.

The ravages of bitter poverty, drug and alcohol addiction, poor education, desolate neighborhoods, and bleak lives wrought by too many Americans growing up in single-parent households seems to have escaped many of us. When some people look at marriage, they don't see that the wives, husbands, and kids live happier, healthier, longer lives, that kids learn more and avoid out-of-wedlock births, chemical addictions, and crime in far greater numbers. They see oppression, misery, and slavery. It sounds unbelievable, I know.

My colleagues at The Heritage Foundation researched just how far some radical feminists have fallen from the movement's noble beginnings as an advocate for fairness in the home and the workplace—which most of us would see as worthwhile goals— to claiming that the only path to happiness for women is to resist marriage and eschew the traditional family model. The history of the decline, summarized in The Heritage Foundation's report by Robert E. Rector, Kirk A. Johnson, Ph.D., and Jennifer A. Marshall entitled, "Why Congress Should Ignore Radical Feminist Opposition to Marriage" is quite disturbing.

The shift began in the late 1960s. Typical of the new breed of feminist was Marlene Dixon, a sociology professor at the University of Chicago, who declared in 1969, "The institution of marriage is the chief vehicle for the perpetuation of the oppression of women; it is through the role of wife that the subjugation of women is maintained. In a very real way, the role of wife has been the genesis of women's rebellion throughout history."

That same year, author Kate Millet wrote *Sexual Politics*, which maintained that "[wives'] chattel status continues in their loss of name, their obligation to adopt the husband's domicile, and the general legal assumption that marriage involves an exchange of the female's domestic service and [sexual] consortium in return for financial support."

Give them full marks for bluntness. But you don't have to be June Cleaver to realize that feminists such as Dixon and Millet harbor an animus that seems almost pathological.

Even after the Age of Aquarius was well behind us, feminist opposition to marriage continued. By 1990, for example, the group Radical Women was claiming the traditional family was "founded on the open or concealed domestic slavery of the wife." (Wait until my husband sees that one.)

The fact is, survey after survey reveals that married *men and women* are happier and healthier than their single counterparts. Statistics also show that more than 80 percent of those who spend more than half their childhoods in poverty live in never-married or broken households. Children who grow up in single-parent households are seven times more likely to live in poverty and six times more likely to go on welfare themselves than those whose parents are married and living together.

Men and women will continue to marry, of course, the claims

and wishes of revisionists and radical feminists notwithstanding. The question is: should people enter the relationship of marriage simply for convenience or by trial? It's time we understand that marriage should be entered with an attitude of commitment, self-lessness, and when children come, we must accept the responsi-bility of shaping the young lives we bring into the world together.

Once a couple has accepted this responsibility, they must pursue the hard work of loving each other. To be quite frank, too many of us are failing to perform this key task to the utmost of our ability.

"I WANT TO BE APPRECIATED"

The letters are enough to make a grown woman cry.

I'm referring to the many stories sent by men across the coun-try to Dr. Laura Schlessinger, Ph.D., which she includes in her book, *The Proper Care and Feeding of Husbands* (and in the com-panion volume, *Woman Power*). After hearing about her book, I decided to check it out because I deeply value her wonderful work on behalf of families. It's so obvious today that the basic unit of our society—the family, starting with marriage—is in grave peril due to efforts by social and judicial radicals who are seeking to destroy the sacred institution, and (what must be called) laziness on behalf of a lot of folks too busy to look beyond the headlines and popular slogans of the day.

Proponents of same-sex marriage often cleverly point to the millions of failed heterosexual marriages in modern culture as support for their argument that same-sex marriages could be more successful than the failed model. If ever there was a time to provide a resource to husbands and wives to help them strengthen their existing marriages, it is now. My original thought was to read Dr. Laura's book, pen a simple, impersonal review, and then move on to another topic.

But that was before I ended up in tears on an airplane as I turned the pages and read letter after heartbreaking letter from real husbands who are berated, relentlessly criticized, and often ignored by the wives that had once loved them with all their hearts.

A letter from "Roy" included in the book expresses the sentiments of most of the letters:

> The world is full of messages to men that there are standards we don't meet. There is always another man who is more handsome, more virile, and more athletic than we are. None of that matters if the most important person in our life looks up to us, accepts us as we are, and loves us even though we aren't perfect. Maybe there is a part of the small boy that never leaves the grown man, I don't know. All I know is that the husband who has a wife who supports him and praises him for the positive things he does is the envy of all the other men who have to live with criticism, sarcasm, and constant reminders of their failures.

"Chris" had this to say about his constantly critical wife: "I want to be admired. I want to be acknowledged for being the breadwinner and making sure that we are all well taken care of. My greatest pleasure is when I feel like her hero. Like her 'man.' Not her boy."

I must admit that in reading the book, I felt a few pangs over the many times when I've served my husband a little too much *whine* with his dinner. Or when I've been too busy, or too tired, or too (wince) selfish to let him know how much I appreciate him. Don't get me wrong, I'm head-over-heels in love with Andy, to whom I have been blessed to be married for twenty years.

But reading the words of men desperate not for fame or fortune but merely the affection of their wives has caused me to vow to let him know every day that I respect and value him and his opinions. If I am to convince other women of the necessity of working on their marriages, I have to face the ugly truth that the majority of the conflicts in my own marriage over the years have occurred because of my failure to follow the Golden Rule with this man who captured my heart two decades ago.

Of course there are some really lousy husbands out there. We all know that. There's never any excuse for abuse or adultery, but those horrors and the horrible men who engage in them are not the focus of Dr. Laura's book, nor this section of my book. Right now, ladies, the microscope is on us. *The Proper Care and Feeding of Husbands* is for wives who have lost their way. Its purpose is to illustrate for women the tremendous power we have on our husbands and our marriages. It's to show us that even the smallest of gestures and words can impact our happiness and lives far more deeply than we have ever realized.

As Dr. Laura says, it's easy to have a great marriage with a decent man. Just provide him with an ample supply of the three A's—acceptance, approval, and affection—and most men will do anything to keep it coming.

Men are simple creatures. They want a wife who not only

loves but also appreciates them. They want to be the hero, to rescue the damsel in distress and keep her and their children safe and
secure and happy. Yet, with the rise of feminism and the "me,
myself, and I" mindset of many women, wives often prevent their
husbands from becoming the heroes they so desperately want to
be and unwittingly relegate them to the status of waterboy. The
result is profound sadness and disappointment for both parties, as
well as for the children they share.

Ladies, if you're married, you must read Dr. Laura's book.
If you ever plan to marry, you must read her book. If you know
someone who is married or who plans to wed, buy the book
for her.

I'm convinced that for every wife who dedicates one afternoon to read *The Proper Care and Feeding of Husbands* and then
follows its advice, there will emerge one invincible and thoroughly
happy couple passionately in love and ready to take on the world.

A CRITICAL ERROR

Shortly after I dedicated one of my WorldNetDaily.com and
Townhall.com columns to Dr. Laura's book, Rush Limbaugh read
the entire piece on the air. In his clever way, he allowed me to
speak to the wives who might be listening. But, wise man that he
is, instead of then instructing women himself, he lobbed a few
missiles at any husbands tuned in that day.

Apparently, Rush thinks a lot of men are wimps. He takes
issue with husbands who complain their wives are insensitive,
bossy, or thoughtless. And, certainly, he is right: no woman wants
to be married to a wimp.

But Rush made a critical error when he advised husbands, "If you want to feel like her hero, feel like a hero. Don't give anybody else the power to determine how you feel about yourself."

There's just one itsy-bitsy problem with that advice. You don't get to be a hero just because you feel like one. You have to do something in order to be a hero. Dr. Laura brilliantly explains in her book that most any decent husband will automatically become a knight in shining armor if his wife stops acting like Medusa. After all, what man wants to win the heart of a serpent?

Dr. Laura explains that when women reject the "me first" mantra of radical feminism and become more selfless, something magic happens: decent men respond in kind.

I've long been a Rush fan. After all, it was Rush Limbaugh that revolutionized talk radio and used it as a tool to sidestep the mass media and reach out directly to the people in their homes, cars, and places of business with a message that grabbed their hearts, engaged their brains, and touched their souls.

I've studied the phenomenon that is Rush Limbaugh. I know that some twenty million people hear him every week. I know that in a single moment, he is able to inspire his loyal listeners to light up the switchboards in Washington D.C. and make their voices heard. I know that he is talk radio's version of a rock star.

But Rush ain't no marriage counselor.

Guys, there's one message you must get if you are to succeed as husbands. It's very simple and is the basic response to every conflict, every miserable challenge that you will ever face in your marriage. It's the silver bullet to a happy household. It's the way to really be your wife's hero. Ready to find out what it is? Okay, here it goes: Love your wife completely and sacrificially. That's it.

Just as you thrive on acceptance and admiration, your wife thrives on *being and feeling* loved. Showing your love to your wife is the first thing you should do in the morning and the last thing before drifting off to sleep. If your wife is a shrew, she can be tamed by gentle love. If she is anxious, she can be calmed by your caress. What women want most—indeed, what we crave from the depths of our souls—is to be truly loved. Thoughtful, simple gestures—like giving her a call in the day just to see how she's doing; or planning a date night (meaning *you* secure the babysitter, make the reservations, and so on); or simply reaching over to take her hand—can make all the difference in the world.

And remember: your children are watching. My Heritage Foundation colleague Paul Gallagher told me about one Valentine's Day when he presented his wife with a dozen roses and a box of Godiva chocolates. His children were nearby, and when his oldest daughter (who was then about six years old) noticed their mother's happy reaction, she gave him a hug and said, "I love you, Daddy. You're so good to my mommy."

One terrific resource to help married men and women is Focus on the Family's Web site, Family.org. Click on "Husbands and Wives" to find a cornucopia of articles, tapes, and books filled with the kind of practical advice most couples need if they're to stay on track—financially, emotionally, and spiritually.

Passionate love is something every human being responds to. It's what makes men slay the dragon and women swoon. And giving sacrificially to your mate—meeting the needs of the other first—is the way to preserve or reignite the passion in your marriage.

SUCCEEDING IN MARRIAGE

Believe me, I know what it's like to be passionately in love.

When I close my eyes, it takes but a moment to see him standing on the boardwalk along the shores of the Mediterranean Sea. I can still feel the heart-pounding, inexplicable attraction that took me by surprise when I met Andy in 1983.

He was the most handsome man I had ever seen, and yet there was something more. When I got within clear view of his sparkling blue eyes, I felt a current run through me, and I knew that our meeting was far beyond chance.

I was on the trip of a lifetime to Israel, along with nine other politically active co-eds from around the United States. The North American Jewish Students Network sponsored ten college-aged Democrats and Republicans on an all-expense paid ten-day trip to the Holy Land.

We met with members of the Knesset, toured Judea and Samaria, traveled through many small biblical towns, and even had a private audience with Prime Minister Menachem Begin. But the most important person I met was a young United States naval lieutenant who "just happened" to be on the same stretch of beach as I, during the same five-minute period, in a country halfway around the world.

We spoke briefly. Suddenly embarrassed that I had introduced myself, I said goodbye and ran back to the water's edge. Hoping he was still watching from the boardwalk, I did what any self-respecting young woman in my situation would do:

I set a trap.

Still in my sundress from touring through the hot, dusty July summer day, I took off my shoes and strolled through the gentle surf. Every so often I would daintily pick up a small pebble and toss it into the waves.

The scene beyond me was majestic. The last sliver of the perfect red-orange ball of the setting sun had just disappeared on the horizon, and the deep blues and purples of dusk reflected off the sea. In the distance, the silhouette of a ship could be seen with its lights seeming to twinkle as the last rays of daylight played across the water's surface.

(Months later when he came to see me in Washington D.C., Andy said, "I'll never forget the way you looked the first night I saw you. You carried yourself so well. The sun was setting behind you, and there was a ship on the horizon whose lights were just coming on." *Bingo!* He had taken the bait!)

Back in Israel, I couldn't get him out of my mind. How unlike me to be so enamored of someone I didn't know. I was still thinking about him the next evening, when, walking through the pavilion located on the beach in Tel Aviv, I heard someone call my name. It was Andy.

Several naval officers and a couple of people from my group ended up going to the movies that night. Afterwards, everyone wanted to go barhopping—everyone but us. He suggested we go for a walk instead.

We ended up walking and talking for several hours, and by the end of the evening I knew he was the man of my dreams. He spoke of faith, his parents and siblings, and his sense of adventure. I learned he was a graduate of the U.S. Naval Academy and that he had always, even as a child, envisioned going to school there. He was a perfect gentleman with a soft laugh and a warm, gentle voice. As we said our goodbyes, he asked for my address: "You're a rare woman. I want to keep in touch."

I was smitten.

And keep in touch he did. The lost art of letter writing was not lost for him—he wrote moving, detailed accounts of his days at sea. The most profound letter described the scene from his ship anchored just offshore in the hours following the 1983 terrorist attack on the U.S. Marine barracks in Lebanon. He wrote of how "the stacks of black body bags on nearby USS *Iwo Jima* grow larger every hour."

He returned to the States that Thanksgiving, and we were wed the next year, in 1984, on the Saturday following Thanksgiving. He is my handsome prince, my knight in shining armor, and my best friend. He is a wonderful father to our three children and a very patient and loving husband. I would be desperately in love with this man even if I had met him in line at McDonald's. God blessed me beyond belief when He brought us together in the most romantic setting possible.

After all these years, I'm still smitten. Throughout our twenty years of marriage whenever there was a conflict, whenever I have been disappointed, whenever the stresses of life have begun to interfere with my relationship with Andy, I have called on the memory of falling in love with him and have reflected on the fact that succeeding in marriage is one of the most important of all human endeavors.

No matter where and when you first fell in love with your spouse, you should frequently recall that moment. But don't forget, mere passion does not a marriage make.

It's all too easy to get caught up in the busyness of everyday life and forget the work that must go into every marriage. Part of this flows from our media-fed notions of romantic love—the idea that a relationship is worth preserving only as long as we're experiencing that pleasant head-over-heels feeling that nearly every couple enjoys when they first start getting to know each other. But those feelings alone won't sustain a marriage; it takes commitment. As Stephen Covey notes in his book, *The 7 Habits of Highly Effective People*, it means recognizing that "love" isn't just a noun, it's a verb.

And it's the most important action word of your marriage. Treat it as such, and you're well on your way to not only protecting your family but also impacting the culture in a manner that will uplift and inspire all those around you—especially your children.

6

PARENT-DIRECTED EDUCATION

When was the last time you looked at your child's health textbook? If it's been awhile, you'll probably be more than a little shocked by the content of sex education—sometimes referred to as "Family Life Education." Long gone are the days of biology class where kids were taught about their bodies and the basics of reproduction. Today's materials include detailed discussions—complete with graphic illustrations—of raw sex in many forms.

Think I'm kidding? Some programs are so disingenuous that their very names are lies. They're called abstinence-plus, or abstinence-based, but they're not about abstinence. They're about the mechanics of sexuality. They suggest teen couples shop for condoms together and mark down the store's hours lest they be caught unprepared. Researcher Robert Rector at The Heritage Foundation tells of a program that lists ways teachers can show kids as young as thirteen "how to make condoms fun and pleasurable." One of the ways to do that, it turns out, is to send kids on a "condom hunt" to local stores. They're expected to look over the various types that are offered and ask, "What's the cheapest price for three condoms?"

The so-called "fun" doesn't stop there. Teachers also are supposed to hold "condom races" between teams of students. "Each person on the team must put the condom on a dildo or cucumber and take it off," the program says. "The team that finishes first wins."

Such programs offer extensive instruction in how to "satisfy each other" short of intercourse: showering together, full-body massages, etc. Does any rational person think these activities make it less likely these kids will graduate to intercourse?

What doesn't work is what the educational establishment has been pushing for thirty years: "frank discussion," "role-playing," and "starting young." Barbara Dafoe Whitehead, an academic who focuses on family issues, proved as much in a landmark review of comprehensive sex ed that was published in the *Atlantic* magazine. She focused on New Jersey, which pushed this approach early and aggressively and has the dismal teen pregnancy and sexually transmitted disease rates to show for it.

The approach is referred to as "safe sex." The defeatist mentality behind the approach is "kids are going to have sex anyway, so we should show them how to have it safely."

Parents should know that this is a vicious lie.

It is a lie that sells our children short. It is a view that robs our kids of the opportunity to develop into disciplined human beings. It is a vision of failure for them and their futures.

Exposing kids to graphic discussions of sexual activity—to what amounts to verbal pornography in the classroom—is also just plain stupid. As the mother of two teenage boys, I'm amazed at the naiveté of those who believe that young men have the ability to listen to detailed discussions of condom usage and sexual activities in one class and then concentrate on equally exciting topics as, say, algebra or chemistry, in the next.

Parents know better. We know our teenagers' bodies are raging with hormones. We know middle and high school years find both genders suddenly obsessed with the ways of the other. We know every form of media—from music, to videos, to commercials, to TV shows—is filled with sexual messages geared toward our kids. The last thing parents want is for our children to become sexually aroused by sex ed lessons between English and European History classes.

Health curricula should teach our kids how to avoid peer pressure and how to practice abstinence—not titillate them with graphic details.

If all of this is resonating with you, you aren't alone. A paper titled "What Do Parents Want Taught in Sex Education Programs?" from The Heritage Foundation reports on a poll in which parents around the country were asked which approach they prefer health classes take. Guess what? Parents want schools to tell their children *no* when it comes to sex.

Nine out of ten parents say that when teachers do teach about "the facts of life," they want them to link sex to qualities most likely found in marriage—qualities like commitment, love, and intimacy. Nearly 96 percent want their children taught that abstinence is best for preventing sexually transmitted diseases, as well as a host of psychological and emotional problems, and for enabling them to form healthy relationships and marriages later on.

Parents want the no-sex message to come through loud and clear. Why? Because they know it works.

In the decade or so that true abstinence-only programs have

grown in popularity, the percentage of teens who say they have had sex by the time they leave high school has fallen from 56 to 48. A popular component of the abstinence-only move, virginity pledges, has produced even better results. According to The Heritage Foundation, teens who take a virginity pledge are less likely to be sexually active while in high school and as young adults, are less likely to become pregnant by age eighteen, and will have fewer sexual partners in their lifetime than teens who do not take a pledge. This should cause adults everywhere to pause and consider a powerful truth:

Teenagers can act responsibly when it is expected of them. When adults set standards of decency for children, empower them to accept the challenge, believe that they can live up to it, and give them tools to do so, teenagers respond.

This isn't just a hope; it's a fact. Consider that today, one out of three high schools teach abstinence-only sex ed. More than seven hundred programs have sprung up nationwide to counter abstinence-plus programs that many parents thought went too far with their graphic descriptions of condom use and lengthy discussions of alternatives to intercourse.

During that period of resounding growth for abstinence-based sex education, the percentage of high school students who say they've had sex dropped from 54 to 46. Teen pregnancy has dropped by one-third, and forty-seven states have logged declines. Students in numbers never-before-seen are taking pledges to remain chaste until marriage. Even a Miss America, Erika Harold, won a hard-fought struggle with pageant promoters to make promoting abstinence the theme of her yearlong reign.

More than 90 percent of adults believe that abstinence

education should be the standard for school-aged youth. But supporters of comprehensive sex ed, the everything-you-need-to-know-to- "do-it" crowd, cry foul. They argue that abstinence ed is unproven, that no one has shown conclusively that these positive trends flow from telling kids to wait when it comes to sex.

Considering the good that has come from abstinence-only sex ed and the fact that, in the twenty-five years before, all those numbers were going in the other direction, doesn't it make sense to increase the kind of education that works?

The six youths profiled by *Newsweek* in an extensive 2003 story on abstinence—all of whom have pledged to remain abstinent until marriage—would say yes.

They would say they learned much from courses where discussion of condoms includes research that shows they fail to prevent transmission of the deadly HIV virus up to 30 percent of the time; that emphasis on condom use over abstinence also is partly responsible for causing the number of sexually transmitted diseases to increase from two, syphilis and gonorrhea, to more than twenty; and that, of those twenty, three—the AIDS virus, herpes, and the human papilloma virus—have no known cure.

Religion inspires many of these programs, and many of the teens who take these pledges do so for religious reasons. But experts told *Newsweek* that, independent of religion, teens seem receptive to a message that stresses self-respect and self-control, which, frankly, relieves them of the pressure of thinking they're alone in holding out.

"This teaches you ways to prevent yourself from doing stuff," Lindsey Rivers, seventeen, told *Newsweek*. "It gets you thinking." Which was sort of the idea.

SO WHAT'S THE PROBLEM?

Organizations such as the infamous Planned Parenthood, which has no moral qualms with teens having sex, are fighting the idea of abstinence-based education. Many members of the nation's teachers' unions also oppose the program. The union in New Jersey even canceled three workshops on sex ed at a convention when organizers learned the three presenters—all distinguished physicians—favored the abstinence-only approach. In Wake County, North Carolina, the teachers' union attempted to get the school board to ditch its abstinence-only policy because of alleged "medical inaccuracies." The teachers failed in Wake County, but similar battles have been raging in Michigan, Minnesota, and Georgia.

Impressive data concerning the effectiveness of abstinence education has been gathered by The Heritage Foundation and is available by a simple mouse click on Heritage.org's "Family and Society" database. The database also is a great resource for other statistics and reports on "social science findings on the family gleaned from peer-reviewed journals, books, and government surveys."

One needs only to review the data of positive changes in teen sexuality to come to the logical conclusion that there is an undeniable correlation between abstinence-only education and teens who are remaining abstinent. It's time to put some real muscle behind such programs that realize that kids can, and do, make wise decisions if adults encourage them to do so.

TAKE CHARGE

Of course, if your school doesn't currently employ abstinence teaching but instead has the graphic garbage that encourages sexual activity, you have the right and responsibility to protect your

kids from teaching that can cause them great harm. Most parents
don't realize it, but officials in many school districts are aware that
sex ed offends many parents and permit them to opt their children
out of the classes. The trouble is, the option is often not made clear
to parents, or is a cumbersome right to exercise. Don't be afraid to
ask, and don't let yourself be bullied. There are very good reasons
for exercising your right to opt your children out of graphic sex
education and to do what is necessary to make sure your child is
not put in a position to be ridiculed or denigrated.

Public schools should give you the opportunity to view the
curriculum and make informed decisions about whether or not
you want your child to take certain classes. Most parents aren't
aware of how bad the curriculum can be and thus never even
bother to look at the texts. Last year, for instance, our local high
school held a meeting where parents could come and view the
sex ed curriculum and ask questions of the health teachers. Guess
what? Out of a school of sixteen hundred students, only seven
parents even bothered to show up. Only seven. And my husband
and I were two of them. And we wonder why today's youth are
having so much trouble finding their way? When only seven
parents take the time to find out what is being pumped into their
children's brains, the central problem is evident: parents aren't living up to their responsibility to parent.

So here's a pointed question: have you ever bothered to view
your kids' textbooks? Why not?

Here's a fair warning: exercising your option to say no to
adults who seek to teach your kids their values instead of yours
might not be so easy. You have to be willing to make unpopular
choices. My husband and I discovered this when my eldest son

was in ninth grade. As it turned out, he was the only student in his entire grade that year whose parents opted him out of the sex education classes. We opted out our two other children also (one in middle school, the other in grammar school), and we continue to do so every year.

Yes, we probably subjected our eldest son to some ridicule that first year. After all, the high school required him to check in each day, in front of his peers, before he went to the library for his "other assignments."

My husband and I take the blame for the ridicule because we're the ones who made him opt out. He didn't tell us until after the semester was over that he had to check in each day—you can sure bet we were fighting mad when we found out at the end of the semester. So, when the next year rolled around, I calmly informed the head of the department that making children appear every day in front of their peers for the simple of purpose of obtaining a pass to the library was an act of ridicule and humiliation and that it is not acceptable to treat children that way.

Guess what? The teacher apologized and agreed that students should be able to obtain a week's worth of passes at one time from their teacher during lunch or some other place when classmates weren't around.

In my case, simply asking for what I wanted helped me secure both my rights and my child's dignity. But I had to ask. I had to have the guts to call the teacher and let her know my expectations. Remember, you don't protect your children because it's easy or fun; you do it because it is right. And what better way to teach your children to stand up for their own values than by showing them how to do it yourself?

Recently I had a conversation with a mother whose daughter attends school with my son. When I asked her about her view of the sex ed classes, she told me that she really wanted to opt her daughter out but had received so much "grief" from her child about doing it that she caved in and let her take the classes anyway. She also said that she didn't know of any other parents who were opting their kids out, so she figured it couldn't be so bad (guess she didn't hear about us). But she's regretted that decision ever since. A few words of encouragement from me, followed with a suggestion that we invite other parents we know who share our values to get together over a cup of coffee to discuss opting our kids out as a group, and a warm smile of hope immediately replaced the stress on this mom's face. A father I know was complaining about how his daughter's class had handled condoms at school that day. When I asked him why he didn't opt her out of the class, he said he didn't realize the class was going to be so graphic. He knows better now, but her innocence has been lost.

An e-mail I received from one mom who read a column I wrote about opting out shows that exercising your right to protect your kids takes some effort, but it just might be what kids really want but are afraid to ask for:

> I am a mother of two daughters, fourteen and thirteen, and we live in New Jersey.
>
> My children have been opted out of sex ed class for a few years now. My decision caused a little tension and concern about peer pressure, but my response was that if I don't stand up to peer pressure now (from other parents) then how can I expect you to do the same when someone offers you drugs?

When seventh grade boys come out of sex ed and say, "Ugh! I can't even look at girls right now," as I observed one day, you know the school is forcing way too much information on them. (I never understood why a twelve-year-old boy needed to know how to insert a tampon.)

Anyway, the result was surprising. My daughters were relieved. Their friends would ask why they weren't in class. When they explained that their mother got them excused, the friends would say, "I wish my mother would do that. Your mom is cool." It is very sad that these children cannot talk to their parents and that the parents are abdicating their responsibility in school.

Thank you for encouraging parents to do the same. It's surprising how many don't know they have the option.

When my daughter was in fifth grade, one mother of a boy in her class approached me with grave concern. "Did you hear what happened in the boys' family life class today? My son told me that the boys were told how girls attach sanitary pads to their panties." She was devastated. If only she had followed her initial instinct to opt her son out of the class. "I just thought that in fifth grade, it couldn't be that bad." It's that bad alright.

In the "Guidelines for Comprehensive Sexuality Education" for kindergarten (that's right, *kindergarten*) through twelfth grade, published by the Sexuality Information and Education Council of the United States (SIECUS), which receives government grants and support, educators are encouraged to teach five- to eight-year-olds about masturbation and homosexuality. Kids ages nine to twelve are to be taught about abortion as a safe procedure and that masturbation can give them sexual pleasure during puberty. Kids from twelve to fifteen are told that homosexuality is normal, that they can buy contraceptives in a drug store without a prescription, and that some kids engage in a dangerous form of masturbation that involves limiting their air supply. From ages fifteen to eighteen, kids are taught that showering with others is an alternative to sexual intercourse, that erotic movies and photographs can enhance their fantasies, that some people who engage in same-gender sexual behavior do not identify as bisexual, gay, or lesbian, and that oral sex is one way to avoid pregnancy.

The point of sharing this information with you is this: in our hearts, most parents don't want our children to lose their innocence in this especially intrusive way that assumes such a cavalier attitude toward sex. We don't want them to be forced to think about sex. We want to do the right thing to protect them; we're just often afraid to. But, Moms and Dads, *if you don't protect them, no one else will.* With a little intestinal fortitude and a little initiative on your part, you can do the right thing and encourage others who share your values to do so too.

THE BIGGER PICTURE

The fact is, we shouldn't have to opt out of sexual education. We should have to opt in.

The government should focus on teaching our children history, literature, science, mathematics, etc. Providing kids with information on sex—beyond a few rudimentary facts that could be taught in biology class—is our job as parents.

Sex ed, as most school districts implement it today, doesn't work.

Programs that focus on how-to information do nothing to reduce teen sexual activity, prevent sexually transmitted diseases, or provide the moral underpinnings our kids need.

You hear otherwise: that we need to "get real" with young people who are bombarded with sexual images, that our only hope is to teach them how to curb disease and pregnancy through condom use, that they need to embrace, rather than control, these new feelings that come with puberty. Malarkey.

What schools should be telling our children in health or biology classes is that sex outside of marriage is harmful and just plain wrong. They should also be equipped with ways of how to say no. This approach works. The growth of true abstinence-only curricula, spurred by demands from parents, is credited with reducing the overall rate of sex among teens from 56 percent to 46 percent in the years from 1993-2003. My Heritage Foundation colleague Robert Rector notes the best abstinence-only programs reduce teen sexual activity by up to 60 percent.

Why? Girls tell researchers the main thing they want to know from sex education is how to say no without hurting boys' feelings. Not how condoms work. Not how to practice "outer-course." Not a primer in the use of body oils. They want a way out, and they want adults to affirm that getting out is right.

"Research does not support the idea that early sex education will lead to more responsible sexual behavior in adolescence," Barbara Dafoe Whitehead writes in *Atlantic* magazine in 2003. "Nor is there reason to believe that franker communication will reduce the risks of early teenage sex." In fact, she says, the opposite is probably true. In 1980, 67.6 percent of teenage births in New Jersey were to unmarried mothers; eleven years of enlightening comprehensive sex ed later, the figure had jumped to 84 percent. And that's the comprehensive sex ed folks' showcase.

Like three-fourths of the parents in one Zogby poll, I want my kids taught to say no to teen sex, not instructed on how to do it and escape the consequences. If your school isn't telling your children no, then I suggest you opt them out. Better your kid be an outcast for a few weeks than the victim of an unexpected pregnancy or STD for life. One day, your children will thank you for it.

IT'S NOT THE SEX ED ALONE

But it can't stop there. It's not just the materials provided in health classes that are offensive. Graphic sex, abundant profanity, homosexual content, and extreme violence also can be found in some of the books children are encouraged to read in school.

Involved parents in California who took the time to take a look at their child's literature materials have provided us with a prime example of just how bad public education can be. They've also provided us with a message of how diligent parents must be if they choose to send their kids to public schools.

Parents of students in a ninth grade class at Colusa High School in California looked over a few of the books the teacher had encouraged her students to read. What the parents found mortified them in a way they will never forget. Although repugnant and offensive, I'll provide a few examples as evidence that it's time for society to say, "Houston, we have a problem."

In the book *Way Past Cool,* by Jess Mowry, one need only get to page four for the first of many uses of the term "motherf—in'," that show up throughout this literature book recommended by the American Library Association. The racially derogatory terms "ni—er" and "ni—erboy" are used, and pages are filled with detailed, graphic descriptions of sexual acts between teens. In honor of decency, there is no way I can give you word-for-word examples. But if you doubt the nature of the book—and have a strong stomach—go to the library and read pages 184, 185, and 187. You'll find enough there to enrage even the biggest skeptic. And there's something about actually holding the book in your hands that some "educators" want your kid to read that gives you the gumption to fight against what you know is wrong.

In *The Perks of Being a Wallflower,* by Stephen Chbosky, a sexual act between fourth-graders is described, as well as sex between teens on a golf course. If you care to see what the fourteen-year-olds were exposed to at the recommendation of their teacher, pages 30, 31, 44, and 45 will provide you with the general sickening idea.

Thanks to the Pacific Justice Institute, this story has a happy ending. The organization succeeded in getting the Colusa County School Board to listen to the parents' complaints. After reviewing the books, the school board promptly removed the list, issued an apology, and is now establishing a book review committee for the school system.

Significantly, when the parents first approached the principal of the school with their concerns, he defended the teacher because the books in question were on the American Library Association's Recommended Reading List for young adults. Educators around the nation, probably including those in your neighborhood, naturally look to the ALA for advice. After all, what are professional organizations for if not to be a source of creative, sound ideas?

But trusting the American Library Association for guidance in age-appropriate materials for our children has become as dangerous as looking to *Playboy* and *Penthouse* for such advice.

Brad Dacus, founder and president of the Pacific Justice Institute, reminded me about a case his organization was involved in at the Livermore Public Library in California that clarified once and for all the ALA's position on children and their exposure to pornography.

The case concerned the library's policy that any child, at any age, should have full access to everything the Internet has to offer, including unfettered access to hardcore porn sites. The ALA supported the library's policy. Indeed, the ALA has backed efforts nationwide to prevent local parents and communities from installing filters on public library computers to protect children.

Sadly, the education establishment and the ALA are cozy bedfellows, and it is our children that will continue to suffer from their incestuous, putrid ideology. Although there are many decent teachers and librarians, the associations of both fields mistakenly believe that they are smarter than parents, have more rights than parents, and are the final word on what goes on in the classroom.

PARENT-DIRECTED EDUCATION

Have you seen that clever TV commercial in which the father, much to the chagrin of his two young kids, gleefully shops for school supplies to the sound of the Christmas carol, "It's The Most Wonderful Time of the Year"?

Even if some parents are happy when their kids head off to school, the dread of returning to the grinding routine is an almost universal experience for children. Which makes me wonder: Could there be an alternative? Could there be a menu approach that would allow parents to choose between and move their children easily between government, private, and even homeschool? Why not make available an array of options for the benefit of the students, not for the preservation of the status quo system?

We hear today that education in America is failing. For decades, politicians have vowed to fix our education system, and more money is thrown at it today than ever before. We also hear a lot of debate about the advantages of a public versus private education, vouchers, and the like, but it seems unlikely that that debate will be resolved anytime soon.

Most people seem to agree, however, on at least one point: parental participation is directly related to the success of the child's education. Since that is a universally held belief, then it would seem that incorporating it to the utmost into our school systems would go a long way toward erasing the existing conflict between the public, private, and homeschooling camps.

Mind you, I'm not speaking here about the timeworn suggestions for more parental involvement in the schools: attend the PTA, help with homework, ask your kids about their day, meet with teachers on conference day, sell raffle tickets, etc. Those may be good things, but in the end they amount to little more than the parent becoming a cog in the machinery of the educational system.

I'm suggesting that we eradicate from our school systems all unreasonable barriers to parental control over each individual child's education, and that we as parents neither neglect our God-given parental responsibilities nor allow them to be usurped.

Schools should be set up in a way that encourages, rather than grudgingly accepts and marginalizes, the concept of what I like to call "parent-directed education."

Many schools have been very slow to embrace the concept of parental control. That may be because parental control over an individual child's learning is often misinterpreted as parental control over the school system itself, which is a different issue altogether.

A public school system structured for maximum parental control would provide broader educational opportunities for all children without having to disassociate any of them from the benefits of the public "system" which their parents' taxes support. At the same time it would allow for seamless cooperation between the currently distinct and often competitive public, private, and in-home school concepts.

Of course, for parent-directed education to work as effectively as possible, mothers and fathers should work together. My husband and I take joint responsibility for making sure our kids are taught in whatever manner is best for them at a given time in their lives. We've kept on top of the ever-growing choices in education and taken advantage of them. We've had our children in public and private schools, and we even homeschooled them for five years.

For involved moms and dads—for those who can and will take the time to truly study what is best for their children each year—the freedom to choose from among those three options or others, such as charter schools, is a tremendous blessing.

The years we have chosen to hand-select the various methods and subjects of study, as well as the instructors and time and place of instruction, are years which have resulted in greater peace and peace-of-mind for all of us. I don't think that is a coincidence.

The simple fact is that I relish the freedom I have as a parent to decide what is best for my children. When I have chosen to live in that freedom and apply it to my children's education, our family marches to the beat of our own drummer.

Unfortunately, income does play a role. I know there are a lot of good, dedicated parents out there who can't do what I do, which is why I'm amazed that the educational establishment continues to fight against the ability of poor families to have greater educational choices for their children. But I'm happy to report that those who would deny families choices are beginning to lose their battle for control.

A few examples of the emerging educational choices that are liberating more and more children from second-rate, crime-ridden schools:

- Some forty states and the District of Columbia have adopted laws that allow for charter schools—public schools that operate free of the traditional public school bureaucracy so they can foster innovation among teachers and, hopefully, improve learning among students.

- Some states have initiated tax credits or deductions parents can use to send their kids to private schools, public schools outside their districts, or for costs associated with home-schooling and on-line schools.

- Many school districts now have choice programs to enable disadvantaged children or kids in failing schools to escape to better-performing private and parochial schools.

How to keep up with new choices in your state? Now it's easy. Check out the nation's most comprehensive record of educational freedom: "Education Choices." This online, free resource from The Heritage Foundation (that can be accessed through Heritage.org) includes much of what parents need to know to make informed decisions about their children's education. You'll find statistics on traditional public schools, public charter schools, and private schools regarding enrollment, teacher-pupil ratio, number of schools, and other data.

The site also contains such measures of student achievement as the most recent results of the National Assessment of Educational Progress tests in math, science, and reading for each state, as well as academic achievement rankings from the American Legislative Exchange Council. In addition, you'll find a snapshot of where school-reform efforts stand in each state and a state-by-state list of educational-reform organizations.

Given the growing popularity of homeschooling, it's not surprising that educators are beginning, albeit grudgingly in some places, to consider meaningful reform. A study released by the National Center for Education Statistics shows that 1.1 million students, or 2.2 percent of America's school-age population, were homeschooled in 2003. And more than five hundred thousand children attend one of the nation's charter schools.

We can all celebrate the fact that there are more choices than ever in every state regarding how, when, and where our children will be educated, giving parents yet more freedom to determine the course of their own kids' lives.

RUNNING DOWN HOMESCHOOLING

I don't mean to suggest that every parent should teach his or her children at home all the time. Although a previously unknown joy and independence awaits those who dare give it a try, my point is that all education should be parent-directed, whether it takes place at home or in a school setting. Educational decisions should be made on an individual basis, taking into account a particular child's needs at a particular time in his life. We've done it all at the Hagelin house: private school, public school, homeschool, and even a combination of all three.

Several years ago when my children were still toddlers, I had the opportunity to work on a public-affairs project for the Homeschool Legal Defense Association. It was in this capacity that I first came face-to-face with the many ridiculous arguments against homeschooling used by the government education establishment.

The PR spin, disguised as concern for the children, usually focuses on claims that homeschooled kids won't be "properly socialized" and that their education will be inferior to those who attend public school. As a parent who has chosen to direct her children's education, I often get the same lame questions every day from average folks when they discover I have homeschooled my daughter. "Isn't she bored?" "How will she learn to get along with other kids?" "Are you a qualified teacher?" And so on.

Part of the reason for their response is the use of the term "homeschool." This simple phrase, for many, conjures up pitiful images of dirty, hungry children watching TV all day. Then there are those who imagine a child sitting in a corner chained to a desk while some evil mother dressed like Saturday Night Live's "Church Lady" stands by with a whip and forbids speaking or smiling.

The truth is that the homeschooling approach to education can be the most enriching experience a child and parent may ever have.

All of the families I know that have made this commitment take their children on amazing trips, experience subject matter rather than just reading about it, join with other families for some study, and have their children enrolled in many extracurricular activities. The tutorial method is, quite simply, superior to any other form of education. A report in *Time* magazine notes that the incredible academic achievements of these children as a whole are outstanding, including average SAT scores of 80 points above the national average for the general population and scores in the 80th percentile on other standardized tests.

Ultimately, it's up to parents to reclaim the classroom. No matter what form of education you choose for your child, you must understand your responsibilities. If you simply hand your children over to someone else seven hours a day, they will be shaped and influenced by those who do not share your values.

As Brad Dacus says, "It's not a question of whether or not a line will be drawn by someone—it's a question of who is drawing that line, and where." Make sure the pen is in your hand.

7

CIVILITY IN AN
UNCIVIL WORLD

One day I was taking a van loaded with kids ages eleven to sixteen home from a night at the movies. When I dropped them off at their respective homes, something was obviously missing as nearly every child jumped out and slammed the van door. It was mildly shocking when it first happened; perhaps they forgot just this once, I told myself. But as the omission turned into a pattern, it became more than shocking; it was maddening.

What was missing? Two simple words: "thank you." Out of six guests, only one uttered the phrase. Let me quickly add that these kids are from good, decent families.

Lest you start thinking, "Honestly, these kids today! They're so spoiled and ungrateful!" allow me to share a similar story . . . this time involving adults.

Shortly after that day, I sponsored an event where I supplied refreshments for a group of about sixteen adults. Guess how many said thanks? Go ahead, guess.

Only three. That's right. Three. (And the refreshments were good, I might add!)

These two simple stories are anecdotal evidence that our culture is characterized by thoughtlessness.

Again, lest you think I hang out with riffraff, reflect for a moment: ever hear of road rage? In an earlier time, courteous drivers meant fewer rude actions and reactions. Ever been in a long line at a grocery checkout stand and have a new register open up? You know what happens: carts go from 0 to 60 mph in a nanosecond in a mad rush to get there first. Ever pull up at an ATM at the same time as another car? I bet you've seen the mad dash there, too. And how many thank-you notes have you received from graduation or wedding gifts you've given in recent years?

From department store "service" counters, to 7-Eleven registers, both clerks and customers lack the niceties of life that used to make life, well, so much nicer. I think it's time we encourage a little human kindness in our own spheres of influence.

I've found a fantastic resource that would make a terrific gift for the young children in your life or for the parents of young children you know. (Note: I never receive royalties, kickbacks, or fees from endorsing products. That would be in poor taste and reek of very bad manners!)

For young children, society's new "Miss Manners" has arrived . . . and she's got great material to help you turn the little darlings in your life into just that: little darlings. Known affectionately as "The Manners Lady" by the students and teachers of the many schools she has performed for, Judi Vankevich has produced a show-stopping, hand-clapping, rousing sing-along CD filled with songs to teach kids from ages three to nine good manners. Each song focuses on a different principle of character or manners. The three themes that are carried throughout the "Everybody Needs Good Manners" CD are the power of showing respect, living by the Golden Rule, and having an "attitude of gratitude."

Your child can join the Manners Club online for free and receive fun reminders and tips for using good manners. (You can find it at TheMannersClub.com.)

Just why am I pushing this so hard? Because you have to start young and reinforce, reinforce, reinforce every day of your child's life to build character and kindness. Everywhere around you, forces have lined up to create a generation that is self-centered, technically oriented to the point of tuning out real relationships, and just plain rude. It's up to moms and dads, aunts and uncles, grandparents, pastors, and the community in general to combat the world's influence and raise children who are considerate, yet strong; kind, yet true to their own convictions; and selfless, yet leaders among their peers.

Folks, as I remind myself every day, the behavior I want my children to emulate has to begin with me. In the hustle and bustle of life, it's far too easy to leave off the "please" in the "pass the potatoes" when gathered around the family dinner table for another rushed meal.

Of this you can be certain: children notice and record. Even when you fear they have tuned you out, kids are secretly taking mental note of how you act and how you *react* to every situation. It might be tough to keep on keepin' on, but it's worth the effort. And believe me, there's nothing more rewarding than to hear from another adult that your son or daughter is polite. Your work and your example will pay off in producing kinder human beings if you are diligent.

BEYOND ETIQUETTE

Want to know how you're doing as a parent? Check out how your children are doing when it comes to minding their manners.

I don't mean just etiquette. How to set a table properly, when to use the little fork across the top of the plate, and where to seat the groom's mother at a wedding reception are only small parts of the equation.

Are your children thoughtful? Do they get up from the dinner table and offer to help with the cleanup? Are they polite and cheerful to other adults they encounter?

No, they won't absorb all the rules by age seven. But "our most important goal should be that they become courteous, honest, unselfish, and well-behaved persons," Karen Santorum, wife of U.S. Senator Rick Santorum (Pennsylvania), says in her book, *Everyday Graces*. None of us is perfect, she says. But we must all strive to live decent and respectable lives and treat others by the Golden Rule—and consistently teach our children to do so. Santorum's book uses a variety of devices to get the message across, the most charming of which is the storytelling from some of the world's great authors. A quick flip through the book finds entries from A.A. Milne, C.S. Lewis, Robert Louis Stevenson, and other great writers.

Take the story of the pansy. (I love how this story includes a word often used in derogatory ways and reclaims its beauty.) "Once upon a time there was a king who had a beautiful garden," it begins.

One day, he went there and found everything drooping. He asked why. The vine said it couldn't grow tall and strong like the pine tree, so it saw no use in trying. The pine tree, in turn, couldn't produce tasty fruit like the apple tree, so why bother? The apple tree produced only small, simple flowers, unlike the beautiful flowers on roses that everyone loves.

Finally, the king came upon the pansy. It had avoided this trap. The king asked how. "I am happy because I know that when you planted the seed out of which I grew, you didn't want a pine or an apple tree or a rose. You wanted a little pansy. So to please you, I am going to be the best pansy I can be.

In other words, the pansy is content, instead of looking for things to covet, to bemoan, to become miserable about. As Santorum points out, "a sweet-tempered child is the pansy of the home." When she comes in, she brightens the entire place. "I've seen a whole bus full of people brighten up when a pleasant-faced child comes on," Santorum writes. One can always find plenty to quarrel or complain over. But why? Why not just learn to enjoy things as they are?

Does this come under the rubric of manners? Absolutely.

The book underscores the strong correlation between good manners in all its forms and strong, attentive parenting. How would children learn to avoid the very natural behaviors of quarreling and whining? Where would they learn to offer someone a seat if the bus is full? How would they learn that their chores are their jobs? How would they learn to speak when spoken to by adults, to say "please," "thank you," and "you're welcome"? God doesn't put us on earth knowing these things.

Children learn these good graces when parents take the time to teach them and to enforce their enactment. Absentee parenting, part-time parenting, parenting that says "Go to your room, watch television, get on the computer, amuse yourself because I have neither the time nor the inclination to make you do otherwise" produces part-time results.

Karen Santorum has produced a full guidebook of the manners children should know. She covers all the bases: how to know what to say and not say; how to act at the dinner table; how to wash and dress; how to care for the sick, elderly, and disabled; how to get along with others and show good sportsmanship; how to behave at school, church, weddings, and funerals; how to handle thank-you notes; and how to respect our country.

It's common-sense stuff, and other books include this information. But Santorum uses unforgettable stories to illustrate her points. She also emphasizes that it's not the rules but the underlying principles that matter. It's being considerate. It's being thoughtful. It's being helpful, generous, and respectful.

In the end, that's what counts. And if your child happens to remember to use the right fork for his salad, so much the better.

AWASH IN INCIVILITY

My Heritage Foundation colleague Paul Gallagher and I frequently have conversations about raising kids. He's a father of six very young children and it's great fun to hear about their many adventures.

When discussing this chapter on manners with Paul while I was in the throes of writing it, he shared a story that illustrates the lack of manners and civility among *adults* these days.

Paul's son, Tim, was going on a field trip with his class from school. But, I'll let Paul tell the rest of the story in his own words: "We received a notice that Tim's class would soon be going on a field trip to the Baltimore Zoo. It contained the usual elements: date, time, list of things to bring, a permission slip. What caught our eye, though, was the last item in a list of reminders: 'Please watch your language when around the students.' As my wife Cindy put it, 'How bad have things gotten that you have to tell parents not to curse around kids?'"

Adults used to teach children good manners, the use of appropriate language, basic civility, but our society is so far off track that now many adults have to teach other adults how to behave decently—not just with other adults, but in front of children.

Whenever I write about manners for WorldNetDaily.com or Townhall.com, I'm always taken aback by how much e-mail I receive on this subject. Seems the nation is awash in incivility.

Take, for instance, a letter from Elizabeth:

I cannot recall the last time an employee or, for that matter, the business owner thanked me for my patronage.

Try holding the door open for someone to exit a store. If there are several to exit, they swarm out as if you are the gatekeeper paid to do the job. God help you if there are those waiting to get inside, for they then rush madly in, leaving the hapless door holder in their wake. This frequently includes the disabled and elderly who are equally convinced of their "right to be served" by someone. Recently I held the door open at a local drug store for an elderly and partially disabled individual who immediately began to tell me all of her personal woes. I listened politely to all that she had to say, helped her to her car, opened the door, placed her package on the seat near her, and then bid her adieu with a "You're welcome" after nary a word of appreciation.

Yes, we've all got stories like Elizabeth's to share. Of course, our natural inclination when ignored in such situations—when we have gone out of our way to help someone who is too rude to even utter a simple "thanks"—is to become angry and stop being considerate of others.

However, to truly influence the culture, we must teach our children to be polite, respectful, helpful, and courteous . . . *and* teach them to continue exhibiting these highly valuable traits even if they *never* receive a smile or thanks in return.

Why? Because it's the right thing to do. How we treat others when they mistreat us is what separates those who exude good manners for convenience's sake from those who are truly well-mannered. If laughter is contagious, so are smiles and warmth. Even the crassest of persons will eventually soften a bit if habitually shown warmth and friendship by one who refuses to reflect their rudeness. And, Moms and Dads, your repeated use of polite words, constant display of good manners, and refusal to become like the culture around you will influence your children. Behaving this way encourages them to incorporate these basic acts of civility into their own lives.

I just love the e-mail I received one December from David in Oregon. It is a great example of how refusing to give into the culture in the manners battle can have an influence:

I drive a school bus in Corvallis, Oregon. I pick up between twenty and thirty high school kids every morning. To each—at his or her stop—I say "good morning" and have been doing so from the start of the school season.

In the beginning, I got a "good morning" return from seven of them. Not being discouraged, I continued to greet them each morning. I now get responses from ten of them!

After I complete the high-school delivery, I then pick up thirty elementary kids. At the beginning of the school year, I had about ten of the children respond to my individual "good morning" greeting. Now, about half of them return the greeting every morning. I will continue to greet each student for as long as I drive a school bus.

Now, wouldn't it be nice if David could drive all of the nation's kids to school? If you agree, why not become that type of adult too?

Constant reminders help. So does a little humor.

I grew up in the Deep South where good manners were *everything*. Children were expected to address adults by "Mr." or "Mrs." or "Miss," and to always use the terms "Ma'am" and "Sir" when responding to their elders. My own father, who was the classic Norman Rockwell doctor, addressed all women—whether they were older or younger than he—with "Ma'am." Fast forward to the new millennium: in the Hagelin household, we still insist on this traditional show of respect for adults. Why? Because we believe that when children are taught to respect adults in their communications, it often transfers to their other behaviors. Now, a warning to any children who may ever hang out with our kids:

all kids of *all* ages must use these phrases when in our home or vehicles.

My goodness, I have surprised many a child who has come home with my sons or daughter with this simple demand. But I don't address it in a heavy-handed way; it's done with a little humor. After all, it isn't the child's fault if he has never been taught respectful speech. My remarks to a "yeah" or "no" response from a visiting child are always accompanied by a big grin and go something like this, "Susie, in our home we don't answer adults with a 'yeah' or a simple 'no.' We use the old-fashioned 'yes, Ma'am' or 'no, Ma'am.' If you prefer, you can say 'Yes, Princess' or 'Yes, Your Highness.' Now, just 'yes, Ma'am' is adequate for me, but it's your choice!"

The kids burst out laughing and don't forget the admonishment. And you know what happens? Because they know that I care about the simple act of how they address me, they instinctively know that other behaviors are off-limits in our home and that manners matter. And my own children learn that it's OK to insist on respect and decency from others. Oh, yes, and there are a few older teens who have never forgotten this lesson from when they visited my home as little kids, who still refer to me as "Princess." Not a bad gig for a woman over forty!

IT'S MORE THAN JUST GOOD MANNERS

Moms, Dads, please understand that this chapter is about much more than manners. It's about the importance of civility, how we practice it ourselves and how we teach it to our children.

Apathy toward indecent, uncivil, and immoral behavior has

been the undoing of many a nation throughout history. Nations who are filled with individuals who are apathetic about how they treat others, and who expect to just be given everything with no appreciation or effort displayed on their part, ultimately become nations marred by selfishness and greed. And as Rome proved many years ago, a nation composed of selfish, greedy, immoral individuals cannot stand. History shows us that no enemy was able to defeat ancient Rome; Rome fell from within when it became morally bankrupt. Common decency, civility, and morality are intertwined, and the future of our children as individuals, and our society as a whole utterly depends on them.

Consider the words of Professor Alexander Tyler, an eighteenth-century historian and economist who wrote the following in his central work, *The Cycle of Democracy*, in 1778:

> The average age of the world's greatest civilizations has been two hundred years. These nations have progressed through this sequence:
>
> From bondage to spiritual faith,
> From spiritual faith to great courage,
> From courage to liberty,
> From liberty to abundance,
> From abundance to complacency,
> From complacency to apathy,
> From apathy to dependence,
> From dependence back into bondage.

Ours is an apathetic society, to say the least. If our children are to have a future of freedom, it's going to be up to us to hold back the tide and start restoring the very basis of a civil society: *our civility.*

My good friend Kerby Anderson, longtime co-host of the wonderful *Point of View* radio show and director of Probe Ministries International (Probe.org), says, "If integrity is the standard we use to judge our own moral development, then civility is the standard we use to judge our moral interaction with others. The rules of civility are ultimately the rules of morality."

So if you wonder how we got to this place of rudeness and crudeness in our culture, just re-read the first three chapters of this book and you'll understand. Kerby is right: a nation's morality and its civility (the way we treat others) are inextricably linked. If we are feeding our children a steady diet of violent rap music, sexualized programming filled with rotten language, and violent video games, how on earth do we expect them to act any differently?

Kerby explains, "While there have been many philosophical discussions on what civility is and how it should be practiced, I believe Jesus simply expressed the goal of civility when he taught, 'You should love your neighbor as yourself.' If we truly love our neighbors, then we should be governed by moral standards that express concern for others. Perhaps that is why civility is on decline. More and more people live for themselves and do not feel they are morally accountable to anyone (even God) for their actions or behavior. Civility acknowledges the value of another person and moral responsibility."

My husband and I are truly blessed to have found a church (Cherrydale Baptist in Arlington, Virginia—in case you're curious!) that seems to have boiled down the basic message of Christianity. Our church mission is "To love God and people above all else." These are the two greatest commandments, and they are shared by both the Jewish and Christian faiths. These two basic principles, if modeled consistently by adults and taught faithfully to our children, would immediately restore civility to our nation and greatly impact the world.

But the popular culture teaches adults and children to do neither. It's no longer acceptable to invoke the name of God in a school setting or to pray for His guidance and blessings. And the price of this secularization of the culture has been a loss of civility and decency.

Kerby explains how the dearth of a common sense of morality has infected our culture: "Consider what would have happened a few decades ago if you misbehaved at school. Your teacher or your principal would have disciplined you. And when you arrived home, your parents would have assumed you were disciplined for a good reason. They probably would have punished you again. Now contrast that with today's parents of young children who are quick to challenge the teacher or principal and are often quick to threaten with a lawsuit. When I was growing up there seemed to be a conspiracy of the adults against the kids. Every parent and every teacher had the same set of moral values. So if I misbehaved at Johnny's house, I knew that Johnny's mother had the same set of rules as my mother. If I misbehaved at school, I knew my teachers had the same set of rules as my parents. Today that moral consensus is gone."

Brad Bright, author of *God Is the Issue*, explains how America has lost its moral consensus in the school setting and the culture at large: "We Americans pretend that God is irrelevant to education, but then we act shocked when our children behave as if there really is no God. If we want children to behave as though God exists, we must teach them that He does. If they do not believe it, they will not act like it. It is that simple." Brad continues, "Morality is merely a fairy tale unless a rational God exists. Teaching values apart from God is like explaining how a light bulb works without ever mentioning electricity, or talking about how the automobile runs but never referring to the internal combustion engine. Talking about values and morality is meaningless if divorced from their source. If there is no God, we are simply arguing about conflicting preferences, not right and wrong, not good and evil. Right and wrong cease to exist the moment God is removed form the equation."

I've spoken about the necessity of every parent first figuring out the biggest, most basic issue of each of our lives: In what do I believe? In whom do I put my trust? Now you know why. Everything springs from faith. What we view as indecent. What we view as acceptable. How we treat other people. How we raise our children. The very survival of our nation.

No, you don't have to embark on a crusade to save the whole country. But by making the decision to instill in your own family basic principles of faith, and morality, and decency, and civility, you will also be protecting your family from the apathy and selfishness that threaten our nation's very existence. Your children's simple words of kindness will be the first indication of your success in teaching these principles.

Perhaps the e-mail I received from Paula expresses best why it's well worth the effort to instill civility in your children:

Nothing gives me more pleasure than when I am complimented about my son's manners and his pleasant attitude about life. Time and time again in school and by people who just meet him, I am told, "He's got the gift." He even makes sure that his mom gets a hug when she's having a bad day (you know this doesn't rate high on a teenage boy's importance scale, but he takes the time to realize that it means something to give back to others). I can't take credit for his personality for it is a blessing from above, but his manners are my responsibility. By combining love, discipline, and lots of patience, parenting is the most rewarding job I have ever had. It's a responsibility that I chose when I became a parent. When I entered into the contract with God, I knew my responsibilities and the consequences of not living up to them fully. I wish more people fully realized this.

So the question is, dear parent, "Do you?"

8

I'M THE MAMMA!
(OR, BE THE DADDY!)

From my lawn chair outside the fence along the first-base line, I can easily make out the form of my son in center-field. Although he is some seventy-five yards away, I recognize his stance, the way he moves, the angle of his shoulders. Line up Nick with one hundred other boys at just about any distance, and I can pick him out in a split second simply because he is my boy.

By the next inning, he has gained a new spot on the field. The coach has called on Nick to take his place on the pitcher's mound. He accepts the responsibility, and in an instant, he is transformed from a gangly thirteen-year-old boy into a young man full of purpose and determination. His stance is firm, his expression serious. My heart swells with pride and anxiety as he is keenly aware that all eyes are on him.

I am his mom, but I cannot help Nick now. From the sidelines, my cheer of encouragement becomes indistinguishable as it merges with the voices of others rising through the dusty evening breeze. Nick does not see me. He does not hear me. He is alone on the mound with only his internal compass, recollection of lessons learned through hard practice, and the direction of his coach to guide him.

It won't be long before Nick leaves our home to face the world. In just a few short years, he will go places where he can't always see or hear me. I know my time to fine-tune his internal compass and teach him lessons of life is limited. But my husband and I are committed to using every remaining minute that God has given us to do just that.

All too often, I come across parents who have given up the responsibility of serving as their children's guides. They shrug their shoulders, roll their eyes, and say, "Well, they are going to be exposed to stuff I don't like, but that's the world." This defeatist attitude is often masked as having an "open mind"—as if there is some virtue to exposing children to a culture immersed in sexual images, self-indulgence, and disrespect for authority. I'm often accused of "sheltering" my children . . . of being "protective."

Sheltering? Protective? You bet I am!

I'm the mamma.

It's my job to protect my children. It's my duty to shelter them from the negative images and ideas that could so easily thwart my efforts to build in them character that is honorable, loving, and dependable.

Children are malleable and trusting; their brains are not unlike blank canvasses awaiting the brushstrokes of their environment. They absorb any image that is placed in front of them. It's my privilege to ensure that their minds are filled with truth so that as they grow older they can easily recognize and discern the good from the bad.

In our household, this means we are intimately involved in the details of our children's lives. We learn to recognize their hopes and fears. We strive to live the Christian life of love in which we believe. We spend a lot of time together as a family, talking and laughing and loving.

Building character also means that before our children can watch a movie, my husband or I first read the review of someone who shares our values or watch it to see if it is appropriate viewing. It means their television time is limited to the stations and programs we feel are beneficial and that they don't listen to music filled with hate and verbal pornography. We guard their access to the Internet, constantly monitoring the sites they visit and with whom they chat online.

Ours is a constant vigil of love. In this modern culture driven by the many wonders of technology, children are vulnerable like never before. We help our children carefully choose their friends and the other homes in which they will spend time. We strive to make our own home a safe, fun place where their friends are welcome. On many a weekend over the years, our home has been filled with pizza boxes, hungry (and sometimes stinky) teenage boys, sleeping bags, and a wide variety of sports equipment.

One day soon, Nick will take his place on the pitcher's mound in the game of life. My job is to make sure that my boy is ready. My goal is to send him to the mound with a reliable internal compass, sound lessons learned from years of practice, and a strong faith to guide him.

YOU BET MOM WAS THE MAMMA!

The family station wagon headed home for what was probably the umpteenth time that day—not unusual for a car belonging to the mother of five children. Mom and I were alone, and for some long-forgotten reason, I was upset.

I'm not certain how old I was. Fourteen? Fifteen? What I do know is that I began telling Mom about some perceived injustice I had suffered during the day, expecting her to pour out streams of sympathy for her little girl.

As we passed tall and slender Florida palm trees lined up like graceful dancers on a stage, Mom surprised me with the firmly spoken words, "Becks, you've got to learn to roll with the punches."

I remember little else about the ride home that day or our conversation. For a brief moment I was taken aback by her lack of sympathy, and then almost immediately her advice struck a chord deep within my impressionable young mind. "Becks, you've got to learn to roll with the punches."

I can still see her resolute profile as she stared straight ahead and became more like a boxing coach than the Southern belle I knew so well. Like I so often did, I adapted Mom's advice for the punches life doles out on all of us. I've been rolling ever since.

As regular readers of my column on WorldNetDaily.com and Townhall.com know, my mother died in 2002. But the advice Mom gave me will last forever. As I continue to apply her many words of wisdom to my own life, I also look for opportunities to pass them on to my own children.

Mom was at once both immensely loving and full of great

expectations for her children. We always knew her arms and heart were open to us, but we also knew that whining would get us nowhere with this incredibly optimistic woman.

My siblings (*four* of them: Deb, Jeff, Jamieson, and Josh) and I have often referred to Mom as the original "can-do" woman. No challenge was too big, no problem insurmountable for her. She was generous, kind to everyone she met, with a marvelous sense of humor and a smile for everyone, even when she didn't feel like it. Mom faced life filled with endless enthusiasm, high energy, and a resolve to accomplish her goals with excellence. And she expected her children to approach the world that way, too.

Although Mom led mostly by example, she always kept one eye on her kids and our own struggles and was quick to offer comfort for broken hopes and hearts, and firm words of guidance when we needed direction.

One particular phrase Mom said to me several times in my youth has served me well throughout my journey: "Bloom where you're planted." I have recalled these words many times and looked for opportunities to bloom in the midst of less-than-perfect circumstances: living as a newlywed in a town where I knew no one, changing what seemed like millions of diapers for my three babies, embarking on challenging professional projects, and serving in positions that were an honor to undertake but in which I felt wholly inadequate.

Mom had advice for every situation. As a teenager just starting to date, it was Mom who reminded me that I was a child of God and had great value, that to give myself to any boy before marriage would tarnish the beauty God placed within me. As a young woman on my own, I remember calling Mom on several occasions when I faced difficult decisions in my life. Her sweet voice on the other end of the phone always gently asked, "Have you prayed about it? Just ask God to show you." And when I prayed, He always did.

During times when I was overly tired or sad but still had work to do, it was Mom who told me that if I would make an effort to force a smile, it would—somehow—actually make me feel a little better and brighten the room for anyone around. It still does.

Yes, I miss Mom terribly. But in my mind and heart, I still hear her voice, and I still treasure and heed her great advice.

THE POWER OF PARENTING

Whether you are happily married or raising children on your own, whether you are a father or mother or a grandparent who is filling in the gap, you must realize the tremendous power you have as one who "parents." You must also understand that the advice you give your children—whether good or bad—will be remembered.

Your power to influence your family's attitudes about the culture should be seen not as a burden but as an innate quality that is always active. You must never, ever forget that it is impossible to choose inaction on your part in the arena of influence. A decision to go with the cultural flow—a decision on your part *not* to fight the culture, to stay away from the conflict and take the easy route, to just lay low—does not negate the influence you have on your children but results in your influence being a negative one.

A decision to not make a decision is still a decision. Inaction, in itself, is an action.

In other words, you are not a neutral force in your household; your action or perceived neutrality is a force that will shape your home and the personalities, choices, morals, and values of your children for the rest of their lives.

Think back for a moment on your own childhood. What are the first memories you have of your parents? If your parents were abusive and selfish, you've probably spent most of your adult life trying to work through all the hurt and pain, trying to get beyond the misery and feelings of betrayal, so that you can give fully to your own children.

Or maybe you come from a family where you knew your parents loved you, but for some reason, they were distant or not active in your life. Maybe you didn't always feel protected from the outside world, maybe you suffered a few hard knocks because they were too busy or too distracted or maybe even too timid to get close to your world and the pressures that surrounded you. You may still be filled with feelings of immense sadness and loss because you were cheated out of the God-given right of every child: the right to have a parent who is intimately aware of the details of your life.

Or maybe you are one of the very fortunate, the most blessed. You came from a happy home filled with unconditional love. You had rules to follow and knew your boundaries. You had parents who were involved in your life, who taught you by example, who were there for you, and who showed you there were right and wrong paths to be chosen in life and that each has irreversible consequences.

Now, ask yourself: Which type of parent am I?

There's no question in my mind that every single person reading this book wants to fall into the third category of parenting described above. We all instinctively know that being that kind of parent will spare our own children—and spouses—much pain and sorrow.

So be that kind of parent.

Today, more than ever, it takes a real commitment to decide to be the mamma or the daddy—to determine that you will take control and be the one that permeates your home with tangible, unconditional love and sets uncompromising standards for yourself and for your kids.

Far too many parents today have morphed into a fourth type of parent, the one who thinks they have to be their child's friend. Oh, there's plenty of love and understanding and loads of fun and games. But when it comes to rules, to setting down the law, to standing up for standards and expected behaviors from your child, many parents today are sorely lacking.

Moms, Dads, your kids don't need you to be just another friend. They need you to be their parents.

And in order to parent fully and effectively in today's media-driven marketing machine, you must be actively engaged in every aspect of your kids' lives. You must monitor their television viewing, screen their movie selections, filter their Internet usage, and guide their music choices. To turn a blind eye, to be too lazy or too busy or too wimpy to take the time and energy necessary to understand the pressures that are on kids today is to doom your kids to a culture that will instill its own values of immorality and selfishness in the void you leave behind. Of this you must be certain: those who seek to market products and ideas to your children are never too lazy or too busy or too wimpy to attempt to lead them down the path of degradation.

As I have mentioned in Chapter Three, you must never, ever underestimate the power of the media on your child and its goal to eliminate any influence you seek to have.

Dr. Ted Baehr, author of *The Media-Wise Family* and publisher of *Movieguide*—both excellent resources for protecting your family—explains why most parents have little or no influence in their children's media choices:

> Teaching children discernment is difficult for parents because they:
>
> - DO NOT watch the movies, hear the music, or play the games that engage their children
>
> - DO NOT understand the cognitive, psychological, and spiritual impact of the mass media on their children
>
> - DO NOT understand how the mass media of entertainment influences their children at various different stages of cognitive development
>
> - DO NOT comprehend the principles behind teaching discernment and media awareness

I would add to that list the painful truth that many parents have become so busy that when their kids are quiet—whether they are parked in front of the TV for hours on end or surfing

God-knows-where on the Internet—they dare not interrupt them. Could it be that ours is a generation of parents that has become so consumed with materialism that we have forgotten that what our children want most is . . . us?

And what about situations that occur at your kids' school that make you uncomfortable? Not happy with the sex education? Be the mamma! Exercise your right as a parent to teach them what you want them to know about sex—go to the school and kindly insist on another line of study for your child during that class time.

Unsure of why your child is forced to sit by another kid who verbally abuses her? Be the daddy! Go talk to the teacher, gently explain the situation, and demand (nicely) that your child be moved.

Don't like the fact that your kids are unsupervised while online at a friend's house? Say to yourself, "I'm the parent!" Kindly explain the dangers to the other child's parents, and let them know your expectations, or simply stop placing your child at risk by sending them over there. If you've set a standard for movie viewing, stick to it. This means coming to an understanding with your child's friends' parents about your expectations.

You must take control, listen not to the voices of the culture, or of your friends, but to that inner voice, the one God gave you as a parent, the voice that instinctually tells you to protect your children.

Every one of us is in a constant war for the minds and souls of our children. Your kids are depending on you to protect them. Read what your children read. Watch what they watch. Listen to their music. If it offends you, if it's something you don't think they should hear, tune it out, turn it off, or drop it in the trash. Your kids may not like your approach, but they'll know you care about them. And one day, they'll appreciate it.

A public-service announcement that started airing a couple of years ago illustrates this point nicely. It shows a quick succession of young adults talking to the camera (and presumably to their parents) about how involved their parents were. They appear to be complaining, saying things like "You were always checking up on me!" and "You kept wanting to know who I was going out with and what I was doing, and I hated you for it" and so on. A pause, and then the kids look sheepishly into the camera and say, "Thanks."

No, it's not going to be easy. There's a reason that Dr. James Dobson titled one of his many excellent books *Parenting Isn't for Cowards*. In this marvelous work, he reassures parents who may be wracked with guilt over a hard-to-raise child or filled with anxiety over the prospect of reining in a rebellious teenager that, yes, you *can* do it—and, believe it or not, emerge with sanity intact. "Anxiety is normal," Dobson writes, "but your worst fears don't have to become reality."

Oh, I can hear some of you now: "I can't take on the whole world!" and "But they're going to see it anyway!" Oh, yeah? Well, it's time to say, "Not in my house. Not on my watch." Guys, it's time to "Be the daddy!" Gals, it's time to say, "I'm the mamma!" It's time we all say, "It's my job to protect my children, because they're just that . . . *my* children!"

9

HELP FOR MOMS

While the rising summer sun chased away night's darkest hours, my somber privilege was to be holding my mother's soft, swollen hand as she left the painful confines of a body wracked with cancer for a glorious, luminous eternity.

Our quiet, final hours together were a unique blessing for me—although I knew the Lord would be with her as she walked through the valley of the shadow of death, I had desperately wanted to be there for her too. I was called to this purpose during what turned out to be her last few weeks of life on this earth; I felt it deeply in my spirit and in the depths of my soul. It became the burden of my heart, and although I made the choice to travel from Virginia to her bedside in Florida, it was the undeniable guidance of the Holy Spirit that caused me to be holding her, loving her, praying with her, and encouraging my precious mother when her spirit was set free from the feeble body that ultimately failed in its attempt to hold her captive.

God called Mom in His perfect timing. I was not privy to His voice, or to her thoughts, nor their conversation. It was Mom and the Deity, and perhaps a legion or two of angels that must have danced and twirled and then flown to that place of perfect peace and abiding love.

For each one of us, those encounters are private and remain a mystery to the rest of the world. I caressed my mother's arms. I placed my hand over her heart and felt the weakening beat. I sponged her forehead, kissed her cheek, and leaned over the bed to cuddle against her shoulder. I sang and prayed and read from my father's Bible. All the while I knew there was another unseen realm of activity around her that provided more hope, more joy, more warmth, and more fulfillment than is humanly possible.

Assuredly, Mom is now in heaven—and I think I've had a little taste of it because she always did her best to make our home a bit of "heaven on earth."

While cleaning out her dresser, I found a letter I had written to Mom when I was a new mother. It best describes the wonderful person that was Alice Faye Redd:

Dear Mom,

To be the mother of two toddlers is a tremendous honor and offers great joy! But it also brings the sobering realization that I am responsible for two little lives and that every word I speak and every move I make can influence those precious boys for good or for bad. Although I'm quite certain I will make many mistakes as a mom, I know I have an edge because I have you for a teacher.

To many women, the word "mom" invokes great fear of the future, or perhaps emptiness and sadness of the past. To me, the word "mom" brings happy memories filled with warmth, and love, and smiles, and security—all of these thoughts are reflections of you!! Thank you, Mom, for a childhood made of frilly dresses, and Sunday school, and birthday parties, and Camp Fire Girls, and good food, and magical Christmas mornings. But most of all, thank you, Mom, for a childhood filled with you. Thank you for always making me feel secure; thank you for always making me feel important and special; and thank you for teaching me that with hard work and God's help, I can reach for the stars and actually touch them!

As a little girl, to have you as my mommy was to have a protector and a helper; as a teenager, to have you as my mom was to have a true friend and an encourager; and as a woman, to have you as my mother is to have a living example and perfect model of a modern day Proverbs 31 woman. Thank you, Mom, for the very special and priceless gift of showing me throughout my life what it means to be a godly woman.

My life's ambition is to follow in your footsteps, to smile your smile, and to clone your manner. I love you, Mom, and on this Mother's Day, 1990, as a tribute to you—the greatest mom of all time—I pledge to strive to bless my children the way you have blessed me. With all the lessons you have provided, and with your prayers and God's guidance, I believe I can succeed. And when my boys are grown and have happy little children of their own, we will all recognize and be thankful that our lives are beautiful and rich because of your faithfulness to God, and your many personal sacrifices and generous gifts of love.

Your greatest admirer,
Becks

.

THE IMPORTANCE OF MENTORS

Even though my mom is gone, I will always remember and benefit from the lessons she taught me. Maybe you don't have memories of a mother who loved and cared for you, who taught you right from wrong, who encouraged you to stand firm against the pressures of the culture and your peers. If not, that is all the more reason why you should strive to be the one your own children look to for unwavering guidance and unconditional love. And whether you have a living mother you are close to, or the memory of her, or neither, all women of all ages should actively seek out role models. Even now that I'm well into my forties and have three teenage children, I still make it a point to regularly call on the wisdom of other women who have walked down this wonderful, challenging path called motherhood.

Modern society teaches women to rely on our own strength and wisdom, rather than on the strength God can provide us through those He places in our lives. Our culture teaches us to compete with other females, to hold each other back; this cheapens the honorable role God has placed on women. Our culture teaches us to be selfish: that life is all about protecting "my body," "my choice," "my career," "my rights," rather than finding true fulfillment in sacrifice and moral strength. I'm so thankful that I have always been able to identify these destructive messages as the lies they are. Not because of some innate wisdom on my part but because of female mentors I've had throughout my life—women I have learned from, drawn strength through, and been served by.

As a young girl, I could always count on my mother to be there for me. As a teenager and college student, Mom was the first to provide me with guidance, support, and unconditional love. She taught me to celebrate life and to deal with disappointments. She showed me the value of having strong values. Mom taught me that I was a person of worth—that to engage in sexual activity would not only endanger me but would cheapen the value of who I was and compromise my future. And she taught me the simple truth: having sex outside of marriage is just plain wrong. She and my dad placed so much trust in me that I came to the point where I never would have done anything to violate that trust. These simple principles and lessons are the same ones I am imparting to my own daughter and sons.

Mom shared in my excitement when I met and married the man of my dreams. When our children arrived, she showed me how to be a mother of tiny, precious babies. I already knew how to be a mom of young children and teenagers because I have such wonderful memories of her in those crucial years.

Later on, God brought four other incredible women into my life who were willing to share their lives and love and to give freely of themselves. These women took me under their wing at different times, helped me find my voice, and reminded me of the importance of putting marriage and motherhood above my career. Yet, they were also instrumental in the development of my own career path. They were all—and still are—incredible cultural warriors.

One of these women, Beverly LaHaye, helped me to succeed as both a mother and a professional. She gave me the incredible opportunity to have a home office—way back in 1987, when there was no Internet and no high-tech equipment to keep me connected. All I had was the unshakeable commitment to care for my baby and a strong will to succeed in my efforts to help her promote the values in which we both believed. Through her leadership as president and founder of Concerned Women for America, Beverly LaHaye was my model for courage, grace, strength, and vision. I still can't believe that amidst her very powerful role in shaping American politics, she found the time and personal interest in the younger women around her.

Later on, God sent another woman into my life who also influenced me in my career, as a wife and mother—and as a daughter in great pain. Her name is Dee Jepsen. I will always be grateful to her for extending motherly love to me during my personal heartache when my own mother became ill with a brain disorder and my world, as I knew it, changed forever. The mental illness that enveloped my mother changed virtually everything about her. From her values to her treatment of others, I saw the sweet mother who had taught me so much about life become engulfed by a person I did not know. It was a great time of loss and questioning for our entire family and community. But a dear woman came to my rescue.

Although Mrs. Jepsen is a fearless leader and dared to take on organized crime through the "Enough Is Enough!" campaign, which seeks to fight child pornography, she also knows how to be a tender teacher and loving friend. And even though she once held a position in the White House, it always seems second nature for her to want to serve and nurture those around her. This remarkable woman helped sustain me through my time of heartache and taught me to be true to my faith. She also reminded me to honor my husband in thought and deed even when times are rough. This simple, often-rejected precept has helped create a marriage filled with more love and mutual respect than I ever thought possible.

The third woman who has given of herself to improve my life is Ambassador Faith Ryan Whittlesey. As the former ambassador to Switzerland under President Reagan and an amazingly brilliant attorney, Mrs. Whittlesey is one of the most giving women and mothers I have ever met. She too came to my aid when mental illness captured my mother. Mrs. Whittlesey taught me to trust in God, to fight for what I knew was right, and to understand that, as Christians, everything we go through in this life is to prepare us to live eternally with Christ. She has also been an invaluable adviser on issues relating to my profession and ideology.

The fourth woman is a public speaker and missionary, and her impact in the lives of individuals around the world has been profound. D'Anne Brown was a longtime friend of my mother's. As a young child I remember how she took an interest in my activities and me. She was always there to support me in my various ventures throughout my life and always had a word of encouragement to share. She's stood by me in good times and bad and earned the affectionate nickname "Auntie D" many years ago. She has gone to China as a missionary, taught at colleges, and lectured on the virtues of womanhood across the country. And she has taught me more about forgiveness than anyone I have ever known. The ability to forgive others is a healing power that sets us free from bitterness and obsession with lost dreams; it is a gift we must teach our children. I'll always be grateful to Auntie D for teaching it to me in a remarkable way.

As noted authors, sought-after speakers, world-class leaders, and successful organizers, I am deeply touched and truly amazed that these incredible women found time for me. They were, and continue to be, my mentors. Although I don't see any of them much any more (we now live in different parts of the country), I know they are only a phone call away.

A DIFFERENT KIND OF STRENGTH

Dr. Beverly LaHaye again blessed me through a wonderful book she authored with former presidential speechwriter Dr. Janice Shaw Crouse. These two women had the vision and calling to write a book about biblical women who have lessons relevant to the modern woman. *A Different Kind of Strength* provides insight into the characters, flaws, and strengths of the only five women mentioned in the lineage of Jesus Christ. I read this book on the train to and from New York to tape a Fox News show. During those few hours, I discovered that even women who don't have living female mentors in their lives do have a place to turn for advice and wisdom. Both men and women should read *A Different Kind of Strength*. It proves that God can work through our flaws, around our circumstances, and above our failures to accomplish great wonders if we are only willing.

In stark contrast to the lessons learned from my mentors and the brave women profiled in *A Different Kind of Strength* are the diabolical teachings of the radical feminist movement, which have robbed our society of many of the blessings God intended for us to enjoy. The embracing of the selfish "blame the male," "get out of my way" attitude by the popular media and an entire generation of women has directly contributed to the breakup of the traditional family unit.

Instead of teaching the values of courage, forgiveness, commitment, and honor, the radical feminist movement and many in the media force-feed America's young women destructive attitudes of selfishness and disrespect for men and each other. In so doing, the movement now bears much of the responsibility for having driven many males from their traditional roles as caretakers, causing much confusion about exactly how they should approach and treat females. A natural regression in male attitudes about courtesy and responsibilities began when the feminists started attacking them. What once was seen as a service and a courtesy—the simple act of a man opening the door for a woman—became an action men had to carefully consider. Soon, the question of "Do I open the door?" digressed to "Do I really have to work hard and offer my wife the opportunity to stay at home with our children?" which further digressed to "Do I have an obligation to stick around and help raise the kids?"

And who is suffering most from the destruction of the family caused by the feminist movement? The young women of today.

All women need role models, and all women need to remember that, de facto, you are a role model to women and mothers younger than yourself.

We have a responsibility to take our role seriously. We need to be reminded that faith and family are the most important aspects of our life and that both our children and other mothers are watching how and what we do. We must realize the power that is uniquely ours as women—that we can actually help to restore America's families by teaching the younger generation the timeless values of decency, commitment, courage, respect for others, and service.

We need to buck the militant feminist mantra that calls women to trash men and husbands and instead encourage each other to love and support the men in our lives. We need to rejoice in our victories and share in our successes rather than being territorial or feeling threatened. We need to be true confidantes, give ugly gossip the boot, and keep each other's secrets. We need to be reminded that power in and of itself is vain and empty; true leadership is attained when one uses her life to lead others to a higher standard.

FEMALE FRIENDSHIPS

Sometimes being a mother can seem like the loneliest job on the face of the earth. Whether your children are still little kids or in their teen years, when you are involved in their lives, it seems as if there is time for little else. Working, dinner, homework, housework—you know the drill—can often zap us of our energy and our creativity. And now you're expected to fight the cultural battle too? The fact is, if you do everything for your kids except teach them how to stand true to their values, nothing else you do for them will matter in the end.

But as I've said before, you don't have to go it alone. Nor should you try.

Look. Seek. Find. In addition to finding mentors, find other women in your age range who share your values. I'm not talking about the surface "let's do lunch" crowd where "friends" sit around and paint a rosy picture of perfection. You know, the "my kids are better than yours" conversations. I'm talking about finding real friends, true friends that share your concerns, your challenges, and are determined to protect their kids in this topsy-turvy culture. I'm talking about finding girlfriends!

Find friends that you can count on to reinforce your values and not undermine them. Friends that will keep your secrets, encourage you in your marriage, and make you a better person. Friends that understand how busy you are, that won't demand loads of time, but that "get it" when all you have time for is a five-minute conversation.

Believe me, they're out there, and they are probably as desperately in need of you as you are of them. I've been blessed with great friends over the years because I sought them out and pledged long ago to *be* a great friend. I've also been blessed with a loving older sister, Deb, and a wonderful younger sister-in-law, Delie, with whom I have shared many late-night conversations about raising children, competing pressures in our lives, and faith. Between the three of us, I have both received and shared ideas for fighting the cultural battle in the lives of kids from babies to grown children in their twenties. What a tremendous resource!

Now here's the hard part. If you have "friends" who bring you down or make you feel like a failure, it's time to evaluate if spending your time in such a relationship is doing more harm to you and your family than good. I hate to say it—but every woman that is honest with herself knows it's true—adult women enamored of the popular culture can often be nothing more than grown-up versions of the catty junior high school girls trying to win a popularity contest.

Do you spend time with women who shrug their shoulders at the culture? Who are more concerned with their child's status than they are with their child's character? Who trash their husbands and laugh about sneaking around behind their backs to buy this or do that? If you are, then it's time to change the company you keep.

My mom used to tell me that when your friendship is true, you don't have to work at it. And she was right. Friendships worth having are those that you can pick up where you left off even if you haven't spoken with them or seen them for months. And since life is so very busy these days, it's important to make certain that the time you can squeeze in for girlfriends is spent with those who understand the importance of reinforcing one another in the battle for our families and our faith.

In a culture saturated with exploitative, sex-crazed media, it's essential to identify the friends that respect your decisions about the types of media your children may or may not consume when in your friends' homes. As a mom who strongly believes the old saying "garbage in, garbage out," I determined early on to say no to those who seek to profit from cramming garbage into my kids' minds. I've found that the very best friends in the modern culture are not necessarily the ones who have a lot of time to spend going to lunch or shopping. Rather, they are the ones I know I can count on to reinforce my decisions regarding my own children when my kids are in their care or in their homes.

Everywhere I've lived, and at every stage of my children's lives, I've always made it a point to know where the "safe" houses are.

These are the homes that I know include mothers whose values are the same as mine. We may not have the same hobbies, or schedules, or even agree on every little thing, but we share the same big-picture goals for our kids. And even if we don't see each other much, we know we can count on the other to reinforce meaningful behaviors and expectations for our children. That is a true friend.

Have there been slipups along the way? Have I misjudged the supervision in a home before? Sadly, yes. But I've always decided it was worth the pain and awkwardness to face the situation head-on rather than to make up excuses why my daughter, Kristin, can't come over when invited. Most times, when I've dared to be open and honest about my concerns, an understanding has been reached with a mom, and I've gained a better friend in the process. But other times, relationships have had to be broken off or limited to situations where I can be watchful. As difficult as such conversations can be, you do live through them, and your child's world is better for it.

When those difficult times come—and if you have truly determined to fight the culture, believe me, those times will come—remember that what most parents and moms really want is for their children to be decent human beings who know who they are and in what they believe. Your tone should be loving and caring and never judgmental. Most mothers these days are simply overwhelmed and don't have the mentors or role models or true friends in their lives discussed earlier in this chapter. The real issue is that most parents don't know how to fight the culture or say no to their kids, especially their teenagers. But I have found that with a little encouragement, with a simple conversation about how important it is to set standards—and to stick with them—most mothers are actually relieved and delighted to discover another woman who will be true to her beliefs. What often results is the recruiting of another soldier in this most important battle of our lives: the battle for the hearts, minds, and souls of our children.

"IF MAMMA AIN'T HAPPY . . ."

". . . ain't nobody happy." A truer saying there never was.

The fact is, Mom, you set the tone for the home. It's been true since the beginning of motherhood, and it is still true today. Motivational speakers who charge big bucks for seminars only *wish* they had a mother's power to motivate, to spawn creativity, to build courage, and to give birth to sheer joy in a household. The true "power of positive thinking" lies in the heart of a mother who understands her influence on her family's attitudes and knows how to use it for good.

Your husband and your children need you to use your power of persuasion to encourage and reinforce them in this most important of wars. Fighting any battle bears a cost. Some people enter battles with great courage only to turn tail and run when the going gets tough. Others would much rather give away everything they hold dear—even their self-respect and dignity—than dare fight the status quo. But most parents—and most kids—will stand up and be counted, dare to be different, and be willing to make sacrifices in the short term for their greater overall good if inspired and equipped to do so. They just need to understand why they are fighting and be encouraged to persevere. And, Moms, like it or not, it is up to you to provide the inspiration.

You must *never* forget that it is impossible to choose inaction on your part in the arena of influence. A decision to go with the cultural flow—a decision on your part *not* to fight the culture by avoiding conflict and taking the easy route—does not negate the influence you have on your children. Instead, this apparent passivity results in a very active negative influence. In other words, you are not a neutral force in your household—your action or inaction is a force that will shape your home and the personalities, choices, morals, and values of your children for the rest of their lives.

Mothers cannot choose whether or not they will influence the attitudes of their children; they can only choose what that influence will be.

So the question is: what will you choose?

10

HELP FOR DADS
(AND A "MUST-READ" FOR MOMS)

The world is tough, and someone has to prepare kids to live in it, both behaviorally and morally. If all they get is the caregiving stuff, you're going to end up with incompetent and dependent children," says Ronald Klinger, Ph.D., in *Common Sense, No Frills, Plain English Guide to Being a Successful Dad.*

Some of you, especially you dads, may think this book espouses a fearful "the sky is falling" approach to living. I suggest you read the book again. Nowhere do I suggest that protecting hearth and home means building walls, digging a moat, and raising the drawbridge.

Above all else, I hope *Home Invasion* resonates with those men and women who are fighters and risk-takers, because standing idly by or retreating to a monkish existence offers no hope of success. Kids who are confident and bold are the ones who will win the battle. The action-oriented person of character who can not only survive but thrive in modern society holds the best promise for retaking a culture gone mad with misplaced priorities.

Dr. Klinger is absolutely right that kids must be prepared

behaviorally and morally to deal with what is around them. They cannot avoid living in this world as adults. As a matter of fact, they must live in the world as kids too. It doesn't work to close your eyes and pretend it's not there. The overprotective approach will not give them what they need. So, like it or not, at some point we must back off from the sheltering, care giving, and nurturing.

THE SCHOOL OF HARD KNOCKS

Backing off is hard, especially for moms. Maybe it's because we are naturally inclined to be nurturers, and, as nurturers, tend to exaggerate danger or have an innate ability to imagine worst-case scenarios. I know I do, and I know my husband does not. Mothers and fathers are not so interchangeable as we moderns would like to believe; both have a vital role to play in raising children.

I could, at this point, relate several amusing stories about how my overactive imagination of physical danger has resulted in late-night 911 calls when hubby was away on some business trip. No need for that, however, because there is a better example.

One day, when my two boys were four and five years of age, I heard a horrendous crashing, screeching, and growling in our basement playroom. It sounded like a raging, bloodthirsty animal on the prowl. I screamed for my husband to investigate, hoping that he could get there faster than I. No response. Finally I reached the top of the basement stairs, only to find my husband had indeed gotten there before I did. In his first instant on the scene, he had assessed the danger *and gone for the video camera.*

There he was, capturing the brothers' tussle for posterity. I, on the other hand, was convinced that this fight-to-the-death put posterity in jeopardy. He had to hold me back with one hand while filming with the other. It took me a long time to forgive him for not breaking up that fight. There was no blood, there were no wounds—only two boys who were roughhousing as little boys are inclined to do. Older and wiser now, I can accept his contention that it was a pretty good learning experience for all of us.

The point I am making is that an exaggerated sense of danger often works against us. Kids should be allowed to be kids. Of course, we should keep them physically safe, but we must allow them to experience a few bumps along the way that will ultimately teach them how to stand up to the culture that surrounds them.

ACCEPTING RISK

Some of what I am about to say may shock you. But first I must point out, and I think you'll agree, that our culture tends to greatly exaggerate some kinds of risk.

Our culture is no longer one that tolerates risk very well. We once embraced it, but we now seem to feel that it should be reserved for professionals like fighter pilots, police, stuntmen, and entrepreneurs. We are a society immensely intolerant of risk, particularly conscious of threats to our physical safety.

Look around you. Within ten feet of your present position you are likely to find ten things that have, or once had, a prominent safety warning emblazoned on one or more surface. I recently bought a stepladder that had seven different warning labels attached to it, each of which was carefully rendered in multiple languages. The lamp on my desk came with four warning labels, some on the bulb and some on the cord. My car's owner's manual contains little more than one hundred pages of warnings about how dangerous operating a car can be, in spite of its highly advertised airbags, antilock brakes, and both shoulder and lap belts. In fact, even those safety devices, like bike helmets and electrical outlet covers, come with their own safety warnings.

This is a mind-boggling development. I can remember playing in the cloud of DDT(or whatever it was) coming out the back of the truck that sprayed the neighborhood for mosquitoes on summer evenings. I can remember flying down the hill on my bike in a blaze of helmetless glory with the wind streaming through my hair. Not long ago no one would think twice about letting unsupervised preteen boys stay out overnight in tents, build fires, and carry knives. Nowadays that sort of thinking is likely to get your kids placed in a foster home.

Somehow we have become convinced that our kids are in danger whenever they are out of our reach, and that they are in *mortal* danger whenever they are out of our sight. Riding a bike without a helmet, petting a strange dog, or swallowing a mouthful of lake water all seem, in the public mind, to be statistically equivalent to a half-dozen turns at Russian roulette using a six-shot revolver. Even dads today seem to buy into the notion that death and destruction stalk kids more closely than they ever have in the past, despite all evidence to the contrary.

Our culture has warped parental sense of proportion about the dangers our children face. We have discounted moral dangers while exaggerating physical dangers. A more balanced sense of these would do more for the health of our children and our society than any government regulation ever could. It's time we ask ourselves: *while we're strapping on our kids' helmets to protect their brains, what are we doing to protect their minds?*

Our kids will only be truly safe for the long haul if they have well-developed personal values and strength of character. We can lay the foundation for values and character in a sheltered environment, but that is not where those virtues will be developed. Character is developed as a result of being exercised through the choices we make and the responsibility we take for those choices we make. If we are going to teach kids to make the right choices, then we are going to have to allow them to make choices. There's the rub. Allowing them to make choices means risk. And risk is very difficult to reconcile with our desire to keep them safe.

Whoa! Isn't that the laissez faire parenting credo? Does that mean "Let them experiment: it's the only way they'll learn anything and they're going to try it sometime anyway"? Definitely not. But it is important for kids to be able to exercise free will; to broaden their own horizons; to learn that life should include some excitement and that expanded independence and self-reliance are the best and healthiest rewards for making responsible choices.

STRUCTURED CHOICES

The male perspective can be very helpful on this subject. As Klinger points out, "[W]hile many mothers tend to be somewhat threatened by their children's growing independence, the best fathers actively encourage it."

My husband's dad, one of the most gentle of gentlemen, encouraged him to learn to swim by throwing him off the end of the dock. I think that's one of those classic scenarios that used to get repeated five million times a year. Little Andy didn't know it at the time, but you can bet that his dad was poised there on the dock to respond in case of trouble. It had its risks, but it was still a controlled situation.

Opportunities to exercise personal responsibility can and must be offered in much the same controlled way. The adult is the one who provides the control—visualizing what could go wrong, assessing the risk, and working to reduce potential unacceptable consequences. It's easiest to do this if you are the one initiating the activity, which is why I advocate that parents proactively create age-appropriate opportunities for kids to act "independently."

So what is "age appropriate"? Fortunately, the physical risks are often not as great as our safety-conscious society suggests. Kids are smarter than we give them credit for. They are also tougher than you have led them to believe.

Beginning at an early age, kids can and should be allowed to exercise independence through structured choices. Options don't have to include both good and bad; they just have to be real choices. Later on, rather than setting up each choice, parents can provide the goals or timelines, then step back to observe and keep things safe.

Chores and allowances offer a great responsibility and reward opportunity. Playtime is also key; the way a kid behaves playing alone or with others is probably the most important measure of whether or not he is ready for more independence or greater responsibility. But in general, as long as a child is mature enough to realistically envision the potential consequences of an action, and is consistently demonstrating a willingness to choose responsibly, there is no reason not to expand his horizons.

Most of us default to a goal of having kids who are making their own decisions by the time they are eighteen. But why not fifteen? Or fourteen? I don't see many fourteen-year-olds being actively encouraged to exercise any real responsibility, even for routine and inconsequential affairs. We lecture them about being responsible, but we tend not to like the risk of letting them be responsible, and we certainly don't force them to be responsible. This is nonsensical. As soon as we hand them the car keys at age sixteen, whether we admit it to ourselves or not, those kids are on their own. We better know what to expect of them by that age or it's probably too late.

This concept of "early accountability" is not something that I just invented. I know of one fifteen-year-old high-school sophomore whose father suggested that he and his buddy might want to drive to New Mexico during the upcoming summer (thirteen hundred miles one way). That suggestion set into motion six months of making plans and earning gas money. Then, carrying freshly minted driver's licenses, off went the two boys. Three weeks later, they were back, safe and sound, with almost thirty-five hundred miles of adventure under their belts.

That's a gutsy call. I'm sure all four parents spent a good part of those three weeks wondering if they had done the right thing, but clearly they didn't make that decision without some confidence in the choices those boys would make along the way. I know that, to those two boys, the display of trust and confidence was an invaluable gift.

When our children were very small, my husband and I began teaching them about the principle of self-governance. It was particularly useful in the years that we homeschooled them. Our little speech went something like this, "Guys, there are many lessons that must be done by the end of the day, others by the end of the week. It is up to you to complete several assignments on your own. You have complete freedom in deciding when and where to do them. Want to do them early in the morning in the treehouse? No problem. Want to sleep in, and do them late in the day? That works too. Do them whenever you want—whenever you're most interested in the subject. But they must be done with excellence by the appointed time. We don't want to be parent police. We want to give you freedom. If you act responsibly, you will have a lot of choices, and much of your time will be your own. But if you neglect your responsibilities and make bad choices, one of us will have to stand over you and make you work when we want you to work until you've learned that freedom is something worth working for."

Guess what? We had very few arguments in our home over assignments. Our children learned that they would much rather have freedom than follow hourly dictates. This invaluable training in self-governance has served our children well. And because they understand it, they now, as teens, have much more freedom than kids who have never been taught the connection between responsible behavior and freedom.

In the summer of 2003, our boys embarked on an adventure that began with a suggestion from Andy. They were fourteen and fifteen, long since recovered from that ugly episode in the basement. This coming-of-age experience was a bike trip along the

C & O Canal with four friends from their Scout troop, all recent graduates of the eighth or ninth grades. The boys were outfitted with camping gear, food, plenty of cash, an emergency credit card, and a cell phone, and the six of them were dropped off two hundred miles away in the hills of western Maryland to make their own way back home to northern Virginia. Daily check-in calls helped us chart their progress, and sure enough, in just under a week, mud-spattered and tired, they were back. After eating everything in the refrigerator, along with several pizzas, and sleeping off the tight muscles, they emerged with a new sense of developing manhood and a clear message from their parents: we trust you.

Mind you, I never said this was an easy thing for a parent to do. It took some convincing for Andy to talk me into actually letting this happen. He also had to allow some time for this idea to settle with the other parents before suggesting it to their kids. Some parents decided that their sons weren't ready to go. Without that kind of parental discernment, the trip could have been a disaster. Letting a child do something simply because other kids are doing it shows poor leadership and can often lead to horrible consequences.

Parents' knowledge of their children's capabilities and inclinations was the common denominator in both road trips. High levels of trust and confidence had been established through considerable experience. This does not happen through occasional observation or wishful thinking. In my sons' case, all of the other boys and their parents were not only neighbors but had closely observed each other through Scouts and sports teams since the second grade. All the parents knew all the kids, knew what to expect from the group dynamics, and knew what the boys would encounter along the way. In short, this trip was actually the result of many years of parental involvement and preparation, even though it may not have seemed that way to the boys.

Those years of preparation were not unpleasant; in fact, they were a lot of fun, just like growing up should be. There were many smaller adventures along the way. Remember, with kids an activity doesn't have to be the world's biggest adventure in order to be a big adventure. By adult standards it may not be an adventure at all, but to a youngster it might be quite significant. Allowing our kids to drive a lawn tractor or build a campfire without a hovering adult nearby show our confidence in them in ways that they will savor and remember. So even though you may want to go along, *don't*. And although you may be tempted to plan adult-size adventures on which the kids come along, opt for the kid-size adventure instead. Look for challenges that can be safely accomplished with little or no adult assistance.

Here is a good chance for me to put in a plug for the Boy Scouts, an organization committed to the moral and physical development of youth for many years. Scouting provides a structured and safe environment that encourages a healthy amount of independence and responsibility while building a strong sense of morality and civic responsibility. It is accessible almost anywhere. It also provides great opportunities for parents not only to observe but also to share in their kids' adventures. Parental participation (from dads or moms) is always welcome, but over-involvement is discouraged. Camping and other outdoor adventures, the Scouts' fundamental activities, have timeless appeal. An active Scout troop will have no problem maintaining a young man's interest. Each troop has its own personality, but it is pretty easy to find one that fits your child's preferences for activities and style of operation. And, although Scouting offers programs for almost all ages, its real focus and its greatest appeal is that period between ages eleven and sixteen, so critical for character development.

YOU, TOO, CAN BE COOL

There is a side benefit to encouraging accountable independence in your child during those adolescent years. Being one step ahead of your child's desire to be grown up tends to make you seem pretty "cool," despite the bifocals and the decidedly dorky clothes. This approach to parenting makes it easy for the child to realize that you are both working toward the same goal. It also demonstrates that mature choices are rewarded while immature choices are not.

We as parents certainly don't want to be all about saying no. You should pick the right battles. As Dr. James Dobson of Focus on the Family says, "Save your big guns for those crucial confrontations. Ask yourself this question: 'Is it worth risking everything of value to enforce a particular standard upon this son or daughter?' If the issue is important enough to defend at all costs, then brace yourself and make your stand. But think through those intractable matters in advance and plan your defense of them thoroughly."

Constantly saying no and building up walls is no way to parent. Our tactic for protecting our children should not be to build bunker-type homes. A far more effective tactic for our homes is to build, in our children, character capable of withstanding the onslaught of the culture.

Besides, adopting an overprotective approach to parenting characterized by the word "no" creates a vision of an unattractive and depressing future. It fails to create a strong, resilient, healthy child. In fact, it practically guarantees failure, producing only an untested eighteen-year-old who hits college or career woefully unprepared, in an environment where failure can be catastrophic. Rather than restricting opportunities, a parent should create them. Provide a vision; offer alternatives. There is no reason why the good and healthy cannot be just as attractive as the bad and unhealthy.

Sometimes we say no for good reasons. But sometimes our *no* response is simply a knee-jerk reaction to even the most harmless request. Always be prepared to say no when it comes to issues of preserving the morals and values in which you believe, or when true physical safety issues exist. But always remember that saying no too often not only gives the impression of deprivation but also sends a signal to your child that he or she is not to be trusted. So say no when you have to, but be prepared to say yes or offer modifications to ideas that your kids present that make both of you happy. Ideally, a dad will establish a parenting style that encourages independence and is characterized by yes rather than no.

LAYING FOUNDATIONS

We have a long way to go if we are to live up to the standards set by previous generations. We tend to forget that as young teenagers many of our own great-grandfathers, grandfathers, and even fathers overcame challenges that we can barely imagine today. Some left home and family to immigrate to a new continent, some supported an entire family or took over a business when a breadwinner died, some went to war, some ventured into wide-open territory in search of fortune or adventure, and others simply put in more work each day on the family farm than we do in a week. Many faced a daily risk of death, no matter how well they performed, and many certainly were in serious danger if they were not careful. Why should we believe that our kids are not capable of meeting today's challenges?

The fact is, all of us—our kids included—meet challenges head on when our lives are characterized by a foundation of faith. The strength of character we all really desire for our children is built by exercising it in the real world, but the foundations of character are laid at an early age within the sheltered environment of the home. How is it that this is accomplished? In a word: modeling.

Okay, dads, I've got a few questions for you: Do you expect of yourself what you expect of your kids? Do you model the values that are really important? As much as you give your children in the area of material items, do you provide that most important thing—a good example?

Dads, a lot is riding on your shoulders, and little eyes are always watching. You've probably heard or read it before, but there's a short poem every father should have, not just on his desk at work but also emblazoned on his heart:

A Little Fellow Follows Me

A careful man I ought to be,
A little fellow follows me.
I dare not go astray,
For fear he'll go the self-same way.
I cannot once escape his eyes,
Whatever he sees me do, he tries.
Like me, he says, he's going to be,
The little chap who follows me.

He thinks that I am good and fine,
Believes in every word of mine.
The base in me he must not see,
That little fellow who follows me.
I must remember as I go,
Thru summers' sun and winters' snow.
I am building for the years to be,
In the little chap who follows me.

—AUTHOR UNKNOWN

MODELING VIRTUES

There is no shortage of virtues that need to be modeled. William
Bennett's popular *Book of Virtues*, which catalogs dozens of them,
is not only a good read but also very instructive as well. I'm high-
lighting about half a dozen of these virtues that are being very
poorly modeled in our culture today. These need to be singled out
for special emphasis at home by fathers. Any of these can be given

other labels, but I have chosen to identify them as Reverence, Commitment, Honesty, Pleasantness and Respect, Fitness, and Communication.

REVERENCE

Your child is more likely to be exposed to diphtheria than to any display of sincere reverence outside of church. Nothing in today's secular and godless society is recognized as sacred or holy. The concept of God, even the word itself (except used in profanity), is foreign to any kid that does not get it at home. Fathers, the impact you have on your own child if you are a man of faith will be immeasurable. In Chapter Four, I shared a personal story about my own father's faith that has served to guide me throughout my life. If you think long enough, you too probably have a vivid memory of your own father's faith—or sadly, his lack thereof—that still lives with you. Both images are powerful; one is a powerful force for good in our kids' lives, and the other, a powerful force for destruction.

Start by examining your own faith and deciding in what you believe. Once you have, practice living your faith in front of and with your children.

It's up to dads to eliminate the profane and irreverent from your home. This includes not only television programming and music that transmit the wrong message but also your own language, and the books and magazines you read.

If you're truly going to fight the culture and raise children who will stand up for what is right, you must teach your sons and daughters that certain language and images are not acceptable.

I never—even once—heard my father utter a curse word. And my kids have never heard my husband utter one. Guess what? Even though I have three teenagers, I've never heard any of them curse either. The power of example cannot be overstated.

As far as magazines are concerned, let me be blunt. If you're into "girly" magazines, throw them out. I once knew a woman whose husband was consumed by pornography. His wife knew it—and he knew she knew—but he didn't care. He was actually shocked when they got divorced, but his wife explained, "Having all those magazines was like having a mistress in our bedroom." How heartbreaking.

Dads, when boys see their fathers reading girly magazines, they develop a warped view of women. When girls see their fathers reading girly magazines, they develop a warped view of themselves. What good father would intentionally implant these distorted messages in his children's minds?

In addition to having your own spiritual life in order, you dads need to add tangible spiritual elements to the family's life. Take your family to church. Being active in a congregation will ground all of you in faith; it will also help you identify others in your area who are likely to share your values. If you don't go regularly, why not commit to doing so? It's important that your family identify with a body and have a place of faith to call its own.

Bring spirituality into your home. This is easy to do. Include some spiritual music in the play list of background music that's on your home stereo. Incorporate grace into mealtimes. Better yet, institute regular family prayer and study. Many good study guides are available through religious publishers. Discussion of what you believe, why you believe it, and how it applies to your daily life enrich these opportunities for family sharing.

COMMITMENT

Most people would define commitment as not quitting, seeing things through to the end, sticking with what you start, particularly when the going gets a little rocky or when something more exciting comes along. The consequences of not doing so can be quite serious. I'm sure that few dads reading this book will be surprised to learn that the children of broken homes are hit particularly hard by the absence of fathers.

Researchers have found a relationship, for example, between paternal absence and the sexual activity of daughters. Writing in *Child Development*, a bimonthly research journal, Bruce Ellis notes that the rates of teenage pregnancy in his study were seven to eight times higher among girls whose fathers were absent early in their childhoods and two to three times higher among those whose fathers left when they were older.

The best example of commitment should be your marriage. After all, marriage will probably be part of your kid's future, and that marriage is quite likely to reflect your own. However, many other commitments in our lives demand our time and resources. Some commitments may actually be interfering with a healthy life and providing a negative example. What would your family say is your biggest commitment? Your job? Your Saturday golf game? Friday night bowling? These things aren't inherently bad, but they can be destructive nonetheless. Your family must know, dear men, that your priorities are your faith and *them*.

HONESTY

Sounds like a no-brainer: most of us think we live a basically honest life. But I suspect the reality may be that our sense of honesty is situational. If no one is likely to find out, or if the immediate benefits of dishonesty are alluring enough, or if the inconvenience of honesty is great enough, we are all in danger of slipping up. This makes honesty very hard to model because it must be demonstrated through its consistent application in thousands of seemingly inconsequential and mundane scenarios. A single slip-up by Dad is sufficient to destroy a good example and to provide all the rationale that a young mind needs to justify its nefarious intents.

Generally speaking, we aren't often presented with situations that call for an overt choice between the honest and the dishonest that allow us to model our "great virtue" to our children or to others. I can think of only one instance in the last twenty years, when my husband found a purse containing over a thousand dollars in cash and returned it intact to its owner, that might stand out in our kids' minds as a heroic act of honesty. It's the daily living, the being true to your word, the being honest in the little things that have the greatest impact on our children's lives. Too tired to talk on the phone? If you instruct your child to lie and say you aren't home, you have not only turned your child into a liar, you have let him know that you're a liar, too, and that it's all just fine.

PLEASANTNESS AND RESPECT

Respect covers a pretty broad spectrum of virtues, but I'm writing primarily of respect for authority, for elders, for the opposite sex, for the feelings and rights of others. Such regard for all human life allows a society to function. In an ever-coarsening culture, there is a real need for pleasantness. Pleasantness is not just exhibiting a cheerful humor but also includes courtesy, kindness, and helpfulness. A significant factor in pleasantness is the ability to exhibit self-control by containing one's expressions of anger and dislike. This self-control is closely linked to respect; it also enables others to be around you for an extended period of time.

FITNESS

Some people might identify obsession with our bodies, glamour, and fashion as one of the great vices of our culture, and I tend to agree. Fitness, however, is a horse of a different color and is undeniably a virtue. I've included it on this list for a slightly different reason than all the rest. Unlike the others, it is not something that is underemphasized by the culture. In fact, I would argue that it is overemphasized. But, despite all the emphasis it gets in advertising, despite all that we spend on health club memberships, we are still losing ground on this virtue just as rapidly as we are on any of the others. In fact, the fitness craze has some interesting similarities to the recent preoccupation with religion: lots of people talk about it but only a few truly make it a part of their daily lives. We've never had so many unfit kids or adults as we have today. Make fitness a part of your life, and your kids are likely to also.

So, Dads, what are *you* modeling? Spending much time on the couch? Are you playing any sports, swimming, walking, or riding a bike? Is the TV on only when you are exercising or have finished exercising?

Think about it! Sitting on the couch for hours watching TV models nothing but laziness. Researchers have found a very close association between television viewing and obesity in children. Basically, the more time kids spent plopped on the couch, the more likely they are to become obese. The tube fills these kids' minds with garbage while they stuff their mouths with other garbage. Studies also show that when kids spend many hours watching TV, they are more likely to be depressed or feel useless once the tube has been turned off. On the other hand, kids do enjoy the active, outdoor things that provide all kinds of health benefits. Getting fit and maintaining fitness are no-lose opportunities to spend time with your kids *and* model constructive behavior.

COMMUNICATION

Communication doesn't often appear on lists of virtues. It's on this one because I'm primarily addressing this chapter to men. Let me be blunt. You men do not talk enough; not to your wives, your kids, or your friends. Most of you don't do a good job of expressing love, appreciation, or encouragement; and you probably don't do a good job of expressing any other feelings either. It's actually a very selfish trait that cuts you off from those around you—those who love you and want to be part of your life.

There, I've said it. Now, what do you think about that? Why not talk to your wives about it and see if I'm right?

A FINAL WORD TO MEN

You can't live a double life and be a truly great father. If you're one man while hanging out with your friends or while you're on a business trip and another man with your family, you're only fooling yourself. Who we truly are as human beings is who we are when we think no one is looking. You're either a man of character or you're not.

Dad, if reading the list above has been painful, or if you feel like giving up, *don't.* Commit to incorporating these principles into your life. If you don't know any men who model the above traits, it's time to get new friends. Surround yourself with those who are man enough to stand up to the culture. One incredible organization designed to help men become real leaders in their families is Promise Keepers. Their contact information is in the Resources Section. I urge you to become involved in this organization or one like it. Your family will be better and stronger for it. And so will you.

11

LEARNING FROM HEROES

The voice was somber and eerily calm: "Ladies and gentlemen, this is the captain. The United States has been attacked. There have been explosions at the World Trade Center and the Pentagon. All domestic flights have been ordered to land immediately at the nearest airport. For us, that's Little Rock, Arkansas. We'll be on the ground in less than ten minutes. That's all the information I have. Please stay seated and fasten your seatbelts."

A deep quiet descended on the passengers like a thick fog. No one said a word.

My husband and I, along with our daughter, were on our way from Virginia to a funeral in Louisiana the morning of September 11, 2001, when terror struck the United States. Our connecting flight was to be made in Dallas, Texas. Of course, we never made it.

After a few minutes of stunned silence, we began talking in whispers to each other. Explosions? The World Trade Center and the Pentagon? What on earth is happening?

A few passengers began making calls on their cell phones. I was the first one to reach someone on the outside. I called Joseph Farah of WorldNetDaily.com; I knew he would be on top of the story. The news he gave me made my blood run cold: planes had been hijacked and flown into the buildings. At least two were American Airlines. I froze—we were flying American, too. I hung up and shared what I knew with the other passengers. Our eyes darted around: was there a hijacker among us?

A couple of minutes later, a man two rows in front of me said the World Trade Center had collapsed. We thought he was mistaken. How could that be possible?

My husband, Andy, who was an officer in the Naval Reserves, was somber. "It's highly possible that this attack included some sort of chemical or biological agents," he whispered. "If that's true, then millions of people could die."

We all breathed a sigh of relief when our plane landed safely. We sat on the runway for more than an hour, waiting for scores of planes that had been diverted to unload their passengers. We were led off the plane into an empty terminal. Airline workers told us to walk quickly to the main terminal without stopping. As we moved down the long hallway, I glanced at the pay phones lining the walls—all were dangling off their hooks. It was an eerie sight.

When we reached the main terminal, we saw a mass of humanity. Thousands of people stood shoulder to shoulder in the hallways. Everyone was trying to catch a glimpse of the TV sets. We were all strangely united in our horror as we watched the reruns of the World Trade Center imploding.

We spent the next five days stranded in Little Rock. I have never felt so helpless in my entire life. Our two sons were with friends in Richmond, and I had no way to get to them. Since our plane was the last to unload, all the rental cars had been taken by the time we made it to the ticket counter. The buses and trains had suspended service. We were stuck.

By the time my family was reunited and life had returned to something approaching normal, I could finally appreciate what I believe is a central lesson of the attack. Like millions of other Americans, I was reminded how blessed we are to live in such a wonderful country—and how we should never take our freedoms and our way of life for granted.

It's all too easy to do, of course. There's something about human nature that causes us to overlook all the things we have to be grateful for until they are either threatened or lost. We complain about traffic, deadlines, and long meetings. We bemoan the party that didn't go as planned. As if there weren't people in many other countries, from North Korea to Sudan, who would happily trade places with us even on our worst days.

Remember, we've been given a wonderful gift just in being born free. Like Jimmy Stewart says in *Mr. Smith Goes to Washington*, we should hold this gift up in front of our faces every day and give thanks for the fact that we live a better life than many of our ancestors did. And much of the credit for that goes to men and women of faith and courage who took advantage of their freedom to build a better life for their fellow citizens.

Some have been famous: statesmen, scientists, inventors, and entrepreneurs who left their names and accomplishments etched in our history books. Others have toiled in obscurity: charity workers, clergy, teachers, and volunteers, known only to the people they helped and by a God who inspires them in this life and rewards them in the next.

And let's not overlook those "ordinary" citizens who go to

work day after day, pay their taxes, raise their families, and live their lives in a thousand honest ways—not because someone's watching but because it's the right thing to do. These are the heroes who make our civil society possible. We saw their spirit at work in the policemen and firemen who plunged into the burning buildings that September morning without a thought for their own safety.

A WILLINGNESS TO SACRIFICE

As long as that spirit is alive, America is alive. To keep America thriving requires the willingness to sacrifice.

That's something Andy reminded our sons shortly after 9/11. I remember exactly how he put it: "Guys, chances are, someday you will go to war." Our family was seated around the kitchen table where we so often laugh, argue, and discuss both the mundane and memorable events of daily life. But that night was different. The conversation was not about schoolwork, or weekend plans, or forcing our then-twelve-year-old to take at least one bite of his vegetables.

When terrorists declared war on America by murdering so many innocent civilians, my children lost their innocence, like so many other sons and daughters, regarding issues of peace and security and evil. And like in so many other homes, the talk turned to war.

I saw the strain in Andy's face and pictured my twelve- and thirteen-year-old boys as the men they would soon become. Was it possible that even my nine-year-old daughter would one day be called to defend our country? Andy quietly explained how those who perpetuated this horrible evil had launched similar attacks on Americans years earlier.

Back in the summer of 1983, hundreds of unsuspecting U.S. Marines were brutally murdered when their barracks were attacked in Beirut. My husband was in the Navy, onboard the USS *Joseph Hewes*, a frigate in the Mediterranean, and he recounted how he watched as the stack of black body bags grew larger every hour on the deck of the nearby *Iwo Jima*. Andy recounted the many other unanswered terrorist attacks on Americans.

Our family was gathered around the table that evening after watching President George W. Bush declare his resolve to find the evil ones and hunt them down. The president talked of how America would pursue the terrorists and rid the world of them, no matter how long it took. We admired the president's resolve and believed his prediction that the war wouldn't be a short one.

My family, including our children, is ready to defend America and freedom at all costs. It is a sickening feeling for a mother to watch the days go by and know that the time is ever closer when her baby may have to go to war.

Mothers and fathers nationwide are grieving the deaths of their brave sons and daughters who continue the war against terrorism. But as in every war for freedom, the ultimate prize is worth fighting and even dying for.

It's a shame that it took the tragedy of 9/11 to make us realize the price we all have to pay for not standing up to evil. Had America responded decisively to the numerous previous terrorist acts aimed at Americans around the world, 9/11 never would have happened. Thankfully, President Bush set us on a course to ensure peace and freedom for future generations, if not our own offspring.

In a 2003 Veteran's Day speech to The Heritage Foundation, President Bush said, "Our men and women are fighting to help democracy and peace and justice rise in a troubled and violent region. Our men and women are fighting terrorist enemies thousands of miles away in the heart and center of their power, so that we do not face those enemies in the heart of America. Our men and women are fighting for the security of America and for the advance of freedom, and that is a cause worth fighting for. The work we are in is not easy; yet, it is essential."

Yes, war is bloody, and our target is often elusive. The lives we lose rip out our hearts and bring the strongest of men to their knees. And although the mission may be long and the path dark at times, to stop now would be to doom our children and our children's children to a life of fear, torment, and subjection at the hands of barbarians.

As my husband explained to our two boys, America must export democracy and our commitment to freedom. Not just because these things are right and just and moral, but because our security depends on it.

Indeed, considering the alternative—sitting back and waiting to be attacked on our own soil—what choice do we really have?

Just ask Gerry DeConto. Or perhaps I should say I wish you could ask him. Gerry, who graduated with my husband from the U.S. Naval Academy, was among those brutally murdered by terrorist thugs at the Pentagon that dark September day.

Captain DeConto was laid to rest in Arlington National Cemetery. Rifle shots sounded through the sunny, unusually warm autumn afternoon in the Navy's twenty-one-gun salute for the fallen naval officer. The lone bugle's mournful notes of "Taps" rang both strong and somber through the clear sky as we stood in silence to honor both the man and his country.

As we stood at his graveside along with other former classmates who had traveled to say their farewells, I couldn't help but think about the many times Gerry had been at sea, had trained to face the enemy, had said goodbye and hello to his family over the years. Who would have ever dreamed that he would be killed, not at sea or during a war he had prepared for but within the borders of our own country, within the very fortress and safety of the Pentagon?

As I watched his stoic, proud mother receive the impeccably folded U.S. flag that had been draped over his gray casket, I pondered the irony of his death. I'm certain that this mom, this wonderful woman who had raised her son to be a patriot, had once beamed with pride at the news of his acceptance to Annapolis. She had probably shed a few tears each time he set off to sea. She had most likely worried about him during his tours to the Mediterranean. But on 9/11, she had no reason to worry: her son was on shore tour, safe within the walls of the Pentagon on duty that fateful morning as the senior officer of the Navy Command Center.

Killed on active military duty in the *Pentagon*? Murdered fewer than sixty miles from the Naval Academy? Until 9/11, such evil atrocities were attempted only in Tom Clancy's thrilling patriotic novels about the struggle between good and evil.

Yet, a few hours before the burial, there we were, in the Naval Academy's majestic and beautiful chapel, attending a funeral that not only honored this brave captain but also paid tribute to the many civilians obliterated by foreign ruffians in freedom's very home.

As we stood to hear Rear Admiral Albert Church read a proclamation from President Bush awarding Captain DeConto the Purple Heart, I was keenly mindful of my own children and how they live in an America that is no longer a safe haven from foreign aggression. I thought about the many little children, moms, dads, husbands, and wives who have suffered the loss of loved ones because our cities became the playground of international terrorists. I wondered, during the moving tribute given this brave captain by his older brother, how it must feel to lose a family member because terrorism has been tolerated for far too long.

Captain Gerry DeConto, along with hundreds of other military personnel and thousands of American civilians, died from an evil that our country should have crushed long ago. The repeated bombings of U.S. embassies, nightclubs, and buses in Israel should have been enough to alert our sleeping democracy that Islam's infernal war soon would be waged here at home.

We waited too long: America became the battlefield.

My husband and I took our three young children with us to the funeral that day. We felt it was important for them to understand the distinction between reality and our culture's deceptive message. Today's culture teaches that anything goes and encourages the self-interested attitude that the world revolves around me and my choices and freedoms. The reality is that what has sustained America through wars past are the same qualities that will sustain us through our present and future war on terrorism: the courage, bravery, and selflessness of our citizens. We must build in our children a sense of duty, patriotism, and honor. The best way to do that is to teach them about those who have gone before us.

A SILENCE THAT SPEAKS VOLUMES

A couple of years ago, my husband and I took his parents and our kids to the Fantasy of Flight Museum, a private collection in Polk City, Florida, boasting what may be the world's largest assemblage of airworthy vintage aircraft. Andy and I felt the trip would bring a better understanding of what Papa John, a World War II vet, and the "Greatest Generation" went through to protect America's freedom some years ago.

Papa John wore his best poker face as he climbed carefully through the bomb-bay doors and into the fuselage, his grandsons scrambling in close behind. But it had to have been an emotional moment for him. During World War II, he served with the 450th bomb group, as a nose gunner in a B-24 Liberator, making runs from Italy into southern Europe. Unlike many, he returned to wed, raise a family, and see his kids raise families of their own.

Even with its bomb racks empty, the bomb bay was surprisingly cramped. Between the racks, the only way forward to the flight deck and to Papa John's former battle station was a narrow girder, not even wide enough to be called a catwalk. Negotiating that, then hunching down, and finally crawling forward, Papa John advanced as far toward the nose turret as his now-creaky knees would let him, just far enough to brush aside a patch of spider webs and peer inside through its double hatch.

He had certainly had a good view from that position, as far

forward as one could possibly be in an airplane, with only a bubble of a Plexiglas between him and the frigid, onrushing air. How had he folded himself, his parachute, and other gear into that tiny space? How could he stay in that position for up to eight hours? How did it feel to be shot at the first time? What did it feel like to climb back in for a second mission? A third? And what did you do to expel the thought that the next mission might be your last?

True to form, Papa John was a fount of knowledge about all things technical. He pointed out the dials and knobs and handles, explained their purpose and how they worked. Those things seemed to come back pretty easily. But how it all felt was more difficult to put into words, maybe even to remember.

As with most of those who made it back, there has rarely been an appropriate moment to share details of those days. Even if the moment presented itself, the story is not an easy one to tell. How does one present the full context of the experience? Wanting above all to be accurate, how does one weave a complete and coherent story out of a collection of memories, some vivid and some vague, particularly when you never knew the whole story anyway? And how do you tell your story knowing that it is only a very small part of a very large undertaking? So, more often than not, their stories go untold.

The silence is part of what makes Papa John—and so many like him in the Greatest Generation—so great. It is our duty, not theirs, to collect and preserve their story. That is why it's good to build museums, write books, and produce documentary films. It's right to recognize their sacrifice. That is the reason we establish memorial days and create memorial monuments in Washington and in hometowns across America. And it's right to thank them by stepping forward to take up the banner of service they carried so faithfully, and by working to restore an America of virtue and strong moral values.

AN UNLIKELY HERO

Not all heroes go to war. Consider this story about one of the rights defended daily by brave men and women willing to put their lives on the line.

I heard this story of patriotism several times during my childhood, although I got few details. My mother used the story to explain what had inspired her own political involvement over the years, as well as a means to help me to understand my simple, but essential, duty to vote.

The unlikely heroine is my five-foot-one, beloved late grandmother, Money Jewell. Money Jewell was an avid Democrat of the Deep South. But more than that, she was an American. She saw the ability to vote as a responsibility that she took seriously and practiced at all costs. I don't think it ever occurred to her, as so often seems the case with many Americans, that voting is a "right" to be discarded at will or practiced only occasionally.

Sometime during the late '40s or early '50s, Money Jewell was diagnosed with ovarian cancer. At the time, to receive such a diagnosis was a death sentence. Undaunted, Money Jewell decided to fight the cancer. She relied heavily on prayer, her belief in divine healing, and the best of medical science that the small towns of North Florida had to offer. Her treatment included an early form of radiation therapy so crude it actually burned her insides. My mother often heard her screaming in pain at night for days after treatment.

During one period in late October and early November, Money Jewell was hospitalized. I don't know how long she stayed in the hospital or what condition she was in at the point of release. I do know that during that era, it was not unusual for an ambulance to deliver patients, still ill, back to their homes. I also know that Money Jewell's release date just happened to come on Election Day.

At some point during the forty-five-minute ambulance ride from the "booming metropolis" of Tallahassee, Florida, to the tiny country town of Greensboro in Gadsden County, Money Jewell insisted that the ambulance driver take her by the polls so she could vote. The driver did as he was requested, and my grandmother proudly, and with some effort, cast her vote.

To Money Jewell, her vote was her vital voice. It was her sacred responsibility—a right bought with blood. Even so close to death, she would have considered it un-American, borderline treason, to leave her civic duty undone.

And there's even a happy ending: Money Jewell miraculously survived the ovarian cancer and went on to live another thirty years or so. I remember her as a loving, jolly woman committed to her family, her church, her community, and her country. She was a woman of simple means. Although well regarded by all who knew her, she held no positions of power other than as a loyal Sunday school teacher.

But Money Jewell was important, because this is America and she had a voice that would be heard.

She was very proud that her only son, my Uncle Walter, was brave, courageous, and served his country as a naval officer. She was proud that he married a sweet, beautiful lady, now my Aunt Myrtle, who contributed to society through the noble profession of schoolteacher. And she was thankful that her only daughter had become a political activist at an early age. My mother registered as a Republican (only one of a handful in Florida at the time); she even stumped door-to-door for Barry Goldwater with tiny children in tow in the early '60s. But the difference in party affiliation didn't seem to bother Money Jewell. What mattered most was that my mother carried on the duty to be involved in the affairs of her country.

Hopefully, Money Jewell will serve as an inspiration for you as she has for me. No matter how busy your day, how awful you feel, or how disappointed you are with the choices on your ballot, you owe it to those who have shed their blood for your freedom to take the time to vote and pass on to your children this necessary responsibility.

Maybe you've never gotten around to registering to vote. Today can be a turning point in your life. If you log on to OperationVote.com, you'll find all the information you need to figure out how to register in your very own precinct.

Don't let another moment go by without determining in your heart, just like Money Jewell did, that you will vote in each and every upcoming election. Your vote is your vital voice, your sacred responsibility, your right bought with blood. It's also the way you choose leaders who reflect your personal values.

Explain to your children that those who don't bother learning about the issues and participating in the simple act of casting their ballot have no right to complain about how the country is run. Ask them: Why do you think we celebrate holidays such as the Fourth of July, Memorial Day, or Veterans Day? They need to know. So many don't.

Consider the preparations that many families make for July 4th: They scope out the best fireworks in town and figure out how to beat the rush to the prime viewing spot. Maybe they plan a picnic lunch or a cookout with everyone's favorite foods and treats. But do they take time to reflect on the meaning of the day?

Freedom. It's all in honor of liberty.

Take a minute to reflect on the many liberties you assume will always be yours. The freedom to speak your mind. The freedom to worship as you please. The freedom to choose how your kids are educated, with whom you will associate, or where you will travel. The freedom to plan your day, own property, or simply go for a walk if you feel like it.

Pause and think about the vast liberty we enjoy because of godly men who modeled the founding documents of this nation on the freedom that our Creator intended for all mankind.

Why not print a copy of the Declaration of Independence and read it aloud at your family's celebrations this July 4th? The authors of this amazing document risked their very lives for its sake. Over the years, countless thousands have left their homes and families to protect the spirit and liberty that document so boldly declares. Take time to talk to your children about and honor those who have died on lonely battlefields and blazing ships far out at sea to protect the freedom we now take for granted.

Even today, as you sit in the comfort of your home or office reading this book, many proud American troops place themselves in harm's way around the world to ensure that we continue to remain an independent nation. How often do we take the time to talk about their sacrifices with our children? Or explain to our children what it is they are making the sacrifices for?

We must remind ourselves and teach our children that freedom isn't free. The rights many of us now demand—like the right to free speech or the right to vote—are too often taken for granted. We must teach our children that these rights came with a price and will continue to require a price if they are to continue to exist. Most Americans don't even know what the U.S. Constitution says and what it means for us. But without this knowledge, it's far too easy for others to pervert it to suit their own purposes. Holidays are the perfect time to print the Constitution and discuss the Bill of Rights with your family.

Sound hokey? Well, remember that the mission of the terrorists who have declared war on us is to obliterate our lives and our freedom. They detest us both for our belief in "life, liberty, and the pursuit of happiness" and for our trust in the Creator from whom our Founding Fathers believed these "inalienable rights" flow. Even when the evil ones fail in their attempts to destroy our lives, they relish the freedoms we lose because of them when we make the fortress walls around us just a little bit higher.

MODERN CULTURE'S THREAT TO FREEDOM

But don't make the mistake of thinking that the only threats to your rights come from international terrorists. Think about the ongoing battles in the public square over our freedom to worship as we please. Many forces in today's culture right here at home threaten to expunge traditional religious practices from the face of our land.

In 2003, for example, just as America's troops were giving their lives in Iraq to protect such basic human rights as the freedom of religion and free speech, the Maryland Senate made its most un-American move to date. Maryland officials attempted to censor the prayer of Rev. David Hughes, whom they had invited to open a session with prayer, because he wanted to end the prayer with the simple phrase, "In Jesus' name, Amen."

When the good pastor refused to delete what is an essential element of a Christian prayer, he was banned from praying at all. In other words, only prayers edited by government officials can be uttered in the Maryland Senate.

How can there still be officials who don't understand the First Amendment? Thank the Good Lord that there are protectors of the First Amendment—the American Center for Law and Justice, the Pacific Justice Institute, Alliance Defense Fund, and the Rutherford Institute—who work everyday to preserve this most basic of American and human rights. The Web sites of these fine organizations reveal so many violations of First Amendment rights it will make your head swim. Particularly disturbing are the many attempts public school officials make to silence religious expression by students.

Take, for instance, a Christmastime story involving students of Westfield High School outside of Springfield, Massachusetts, brought to court by the Liberty Council in Orlando, Florida. A few kids asked their principal if they could distribute candy canes that had a Christian message attached. The principal refused. The school superintendent was also approached and the same *no* was given. Why? Because the administration feared that the message on the attached cards "might offend" other students. The simple words of "Merry Christmas" were deemed too religious.

The kids, taking their orders from a little higher up, disobeyed the principal and handed out four hundred and fifty candy canes the day before Christmas break. The principal ordered in-school suspensions for ignoring his orders. Six of the seven refused to accept the punishment and took him to court. Thankfully, a federal judge ruled in their favor.

Because the candy canes might offend students? In this case, the principal and superintendent were acting as agents of the state. If it's going to be the position of the state of Massachusetts—or any other state—that anything that "might offend" someone will be forbidden from the public square, then here are a few items we might ban:

- Triple-X movie theaters? See ya!
- "Piss Christ" and any number of its cousins in the thoroughly unoriginal, incredibly irreligious shock-schlock genre of postmodern art? Bon voyage!
- Shock jocks? Pull the plug!

The truth is, our culture is chock-full of images today that offend large swaths of the population. In some cases, such as the aforementioned postmodern art, those large swaths are even asked to pay for the offensive material.

Is it right to ask the government to ban such images and items that even most Americans find offensive? In cases of indecency, the Supreme Court has said yes. But in most cases, no. The best we can do as parents is to teach our children right from wrong and trust that they, too, know to turn away when they see so much of what our "culture" has to offer.

But let a kid put down his violent video games and his bong and his F-word-loaded rap music and take up the cause of spreading the word of Christ and suddenly school officials everywhere are worried whether their conduct "might offend" people.

Ah, some say, but those movies and commercials and reality shows and rappers are protected by the First Amendment. Well, guess what? So are the candy cane kids and the pastor in Maryland. As our brave soldiers battle overseas for the rights of the oppressed, we must remember that free speech and the freedom of religion are bedrock principles that are worth fighting for, whether through the courts here at home or on a battlefield far away.

"ARMIES" ALL AROUND US

Not all of us, of course, can serve in the military. But that doesn't mean we can't serve our country with distinction. Indeed, armies exist all around you. These are the men and women who work to uplift people in their communities—those who are poor in body (the homeless, the addicts), as well as those who are poor in spirit (the depressed, the abused).

This impulse to help one's fellow neighbor is a deeply ingrained characteristic of the American psyche, one that flows naturally from our unique outlook. Those who think that liberals have a lock on compassion may be surprised to learn that it flourishes best under what is widely considered a conservative goal: limited government.

"I often admired the infinite art with which the inhabitants of the United States managed to fix a common goal to the efforts of many men and to get them to advance it freely," Alexis de Tocqueville wrote in *Democracy in America*. "What political power could ever be in a state to suffice for the innumerable multitude of small undertakings that American citizens execute every day with the aid of an association?"

As my Heritage Foundation colleague Matthew Spalding, an expert on the Founding Fathers, has pointed out, those "associations," from schools and churches to hospitals and charities, sustain the social order and encourage morality. They draw us out of the pursuit of our own selfish goals and "cultivate the personal character that is the foundation of a self-governing society," he writes in the Heritage paper, "Principles and Reforms for Citizen Service."

Who forces men and women to join these associations and serve the poor and destitute? No one. And that's part of the greatness of American society. Countless heroes are out there every day doing the job of lifting up their downtrodden brethren. They aren't doing it because the government told them to do it. The vast majority of them are motivated by something far more influential than a government paycheck: the love of a God that urges them to treat all men and women with compassion. They're motivated not by love of money but by love itself.

Spalding notes that in 2001, 83.9 million adults volunteered time to a formal charity organization, and 89 percent of American households together gave a total of $212 billion to charity. That same year, the Knights of Columbus alone raised and distributed $125.6 million (half the AmeriCorps budget) and volunteered 58 million hours of service (almost 90 percent of AmeriCorps participants' service time). "These private voluntary organizations thrive today precisely because their work is privately organized, highly decentralized, and directly focused on community needs and local conditions," he writes.

Think of the good that you can accomplish and the impact you can have on your local culture if you encourage your children to commit their time and effort to helping someone who's needy. Of course, the best way to do that is by example. It doesn't take a major time commitment. Ask your pastor if there's something you can do. Even one or two hours a week, whether it's teaching a literacy class or counseling young people who have no positive role models, can make a difference. And think: you'll be connecting yourself to the spirit that founded this country, the spirit that makes America a beacon for the rest of the world.

"The preservation of the sacred fire of liberty, and the destiny of the republican model of government," George Washington wrote in his First Inaugural Address, "are justly considered as deeply, perhaps as finally, staked on the experiment entrusted to the hands of the American people." That means you and me. We've been handed a great gift, but we have a trust to keep. Will we let others down? Or will we deliver the service we all know we're capable of giving?

12

COACHING FOR LIFE

My first order of business upon arriving at the track meet on that sunny spring morning was to find Nick. From my perch on the metal bleachers, I scanned the vast field for my son. Like confetti blowing in the wind, the colorful array of school uniforms and constant movement of the hundreds of athletes across the football field and around the massive track warming up for the various events made it a real challenge to locate him. *Okay*, I thought, *I'll never find him this way. I should look for athletes preparing for the long jump, his first event.*

Across the field and to the left, I spotted a steady stream of tiny figures running swiftly for a brief distance and then lifting into the air. Within seconds, a familiar physique caught my eye as it sprinted down the short track and took flight. I had found my son.

I quickly decided to cross the field and find a better vantage point for watching him compete. Within a couple of minutes, I arrived at a small strip of grass next to the sand pit just in time for Nick to make another practice run. As other athletes warmed up nearby, the morning air was punctuated with last minute tips from coaches and teammates. "Measure your steps," one said.

"Don't forget to look for your mark," yelled another. But I knew the last-minute coaching alone would not determine the day's champions. It was the months of intense training—the sweat, the countless hours of running, lifting weights, and practicing techniques that would define the winners of the day. The precise steps, careful pacing, measured approach, angle of the jump, and strength of the body were skills and assets that could not be mastered at the last minute.

As I proudly watched the tall, muscular, disciplined young man that had once been the helpless little baby cradled in my arms, it dawned on me that my most important role in life has been as Nick's coach.

No, not the coach who taught him the skills necessary to do his very best in the long and high jump but the coach who has concentrated on teaching him the skills necessary to do his very best in life. Correction: the coach who is *still* teaching him how to stand up for what is right, how to live out loyalty and friendship, generosity, hard work, and sacrifice. I am coaching him to know that truth must never be compromised and teaching him about the absolute necessity of choosing whom he will serve: God or man.

I thought about the utter futility of the last-minute efforts of some parents who, like the exhausted, whipped coach at the end of a losing season, have grown weary of fighting the culture and relinquished their roles as trainers, passing off the responsibility of daily training their teens to schoolteachers, the media, or their drifting peers.

My time at the track meet on that morning poignantly reminded me that parenting is not a part-time job. I cannot give up or tire out in the responsibility to use every day to coach my children in values and virtues. In so doing, I will establish them both as productive members of society and as souls who will answer eternally for the decisions they make and the love they share. Yes, parents should enthusiastically give last-minute reminders to children before milestone events in their lives— reminders like "Measure your steps" and "Don't forget to look for your mark" are crucial. But, just like the words of a coach on the day of the big meet, our advice in those key moments will be truly effective only if they are based on a foundation of character development to which we have committed ourselves day in and day out through their childhood.

Why is it that so many parents are great at teaching kids about sports, or the importance of homework, or how to make the most of their talents, yet are not so committed when it comes to coaching for character? So many of the same principles can apply to teaching our kids about morals and values. Just as a child needs to be coached on the field to improve his game, our sons and daughters must be coached in life to build their character.

Even if, while reading this book, you realize you are starting late in the game, please don't give up. Seize every minute, find reinforcements, gather all the resources you can, and quickly establish your family in faith, in unconditional love, and in open communication. Reclaim your role as parent through admitting both your past failures and your new resolve to coach your child in unconditional principles and unconditional love. Never forget we have a limited time in which to mold our children's hearts.

My children have always depended on my husband and me for guidance, moral training, and love. Our two fine boys have spent their lives—like all boys do—always watching, always seeking, always being influenced.

Even though they are now in high school, every day we work to instill in them honesty, integrity, compassion, commitment, dependability, patriotism, and respect for others. Our friends are families who share our values. They are active in the church youth group. They are members of the Boy Scouts, and my husband even served several years as the scoutmaster. We carefully screen the movies they go to, the video games they play, and the television they watch. Our computer sits in a common room in full view where Internet access can be monitored. My husband and I— keenly aware that children usually model their future marriages after their parents' relationships—love each other with visible warmth and affection. We also try our very best to live our faith.

MODELING RAUNCHY BEHAVIOR

On many weekends, our home is bursting with boys, their stinky socks and sleeping bags, pizza boxes, innocent pranks, and laughter. We have created a safe and nurturing environment for our sons and their friends. When they were younger, we even had a three-story treehouse in the backyard that my husband and boys designed and built together, a fire pit for weekend campfires, and a swinging bridge that hangs between two towering oaks.

But we still struggle every day with the negative influence of our culture. Funny thing is, it's not the products Hollywood produces that are the biggest threat to our boys anymore. The most ominous threat these days comes from the male "leaders" in the world of sports, entertainment, and even in our nation's capital.

How sad that the rich and famous—men that many boys look up to as heroes—have forgotten the tremendous influence they have on our country's sons. How dreadful that the nightly news must be filled with stories of illicit affairs, family betrayal, deceit, lies, and graphic sexual encounters. How sickening that the political pundits try to spin these destructive forces as issues of "privacy" and "free will" and "personal choice." If I hear one more time that a "public figure's personal life is no one else's business," I'm going to scream. Unfortunately, you'll probably hear me within the hour.

This can be a painful job. For instance, we had to grapple with the sordid behavior discussed daily on the news about basketball star Kobe Bryant and his alleged rape of a young woman he had just met. While the criminal charges against the famous athlete were eventually dropped, what was clear from the very beginning was that this tall, good-looking, all-American role model had cheated on his wife in what he claims was a mere "one night stand." America was subjected to a blow-by-blow account of the despicable drama for months on end.

And who can forget the equally sordid story about Congressman Gary Condit who denied then admitted to having an affair with a young intern later found murdered? (It's important to note that although the Congressman is not a suspect in this still unsolved murder, he fell under a cloud of suspicion when it was discovered he was having an affair with the missing girl.) This story followed on the heels of the biggest presidential scandal of this generation. I'll never forget how awful it was to tell our boys that the then-president of the United States should no longer be considered a role model. Almost nightly, we discussed why Clinton was the exact opposite of the type of husband, father, and moral leader we would like for them to be. My heart was in my throat as I looked into their confused and inquisitive faces. It seemed so very wrong to have to say such things about the president of the United States.

And then it got worse: the president got away with it. The spin machine won over decency. Most parents I know—regardless of their political persuasion—were embarrassed by Clinton's actions. But pundits and mass media seemed to care more about their politics than an entire generation of young men. Hillary smiled and waved, the president lied to reporters and you and me, and his supporters continued to publicly acclaim their man.

Of course, numerous other scandals involving many of our nation's leaders and sports stars have surfaced throughout our kids' childhoods. Why do so many successful men at the top of their careers fail miserably when it comes to character and their personal lives?

Seedy sex, betrayal, and lies are often the behaviors practiced by so many who dominate and lead various elements of our culture. How can this be? It's agony to try and make sense of it for my boys, because it is senseless. A president and congressman who felt no obligation to their wives and families? Leaders who hold no regard for their influence on our nation's sons? These men were too busy building their personal empires of fame, fortune, and power to stop and look into the seeking eyes of America's young men.

And then there are the women.

The women involved in all of the above affairs are culpable as well. Kobe Bryant's accuser—who admitted to having sex with other men within hours of the Bryant incident, and whose identity the court "mistakenly" revealed—will spend the rest of her life working through shame and public scorn. The young intern, Chandra Levy, will always be known both for her mysterious death and her affair with a powerful congressman. And the name Monica Lewinsky will forever be synonymous with the sexual act she performed on the president of the United States.

No doubt, none of these women would have been known to the public had they not carried on with famous, powerful, wealthy men. They broke the rules of decency and got caught— and they all paid dearly. Although heartbreaking for their families, the message to America's daughters is very clear: be sure, your sins will find you out.

Or will they?

What about the female images the entertainment and advertising industries hold up for our young girls to emulate? They run around scantily clad, engaging in illicit sex and spouting foul language; yet they seem to have all the fun, fortune, and fame a girl could want.

I'm very sad for my thirteen-year-old daughter. The female images of success that are held before her by the popular culture are hollow and superficial. It seems the only repeat message that is offered her is this: be a beautiful sex object and you've got it made.

Sadly, I'm sure you know what I'm talking about.

Ever try finding an admirable female image when walking through the mall? The larger-than-life posters that fill the windows of virtually every store—from clothing, to music, to jewelry stores—contain images of nearly naked, anorexic young girls made up to look like prostitutes. What does this constant display of female sexuality and unhealthy bodies do to the psyches of America's little girls?

And what about the teen magazines? One study by the Simmons Market Research Bureau revealed that magazines are wildly popular with today's youth, but while teen boys read magazines mostly for sports or gaming information, girls read them for information on fashion and beauty. In other words, girls are purchasing the magazines to learn something about beauty and style that they can incorporate into their lives. So what are the magazines teaching them?

According to researchers referenced in a study called the "Impact of the Media on Adolescent Sexual Attitudes and Behaviors" produced by the Medical Institute in Austin, Texas, "Teen girl magazines include an average of one to six articles per issue on sexual topics. Content analysis indicates that magazines aimed at teen girls (including young teens) provide messages that girls should be beautiful and plan their lives to attract a man, depict girls as sexual objects, and display nudity in fashions, and sexual explicitness through the exposure of girls' breasts, buttocks, and genitals."

Of course, it doesn't take reading mounds of research to know the above is true. Any mom or dad can casually flip through the pages of popular teen magazines at the checkout stand and quickly see the pressures that are being put on our daughters.

Which brings me to a very sensitive question for the moms reading this book: Do you read the trash too?

Your daughters are watching.

They know when you are reading garbage in your own women's magazine while planted on the couch. They observe you picking up the magazines with screaming headlines like "Best Sex Ever!" "What He Really Wants in Bed," and "Be a Sex Diva" on the cover while waiting to see the dentist or relaxing on vacation. Be careful what you model, Mom: if you're consumed by the media manipulators, your daughter doesn't stand a chance. You must remember that the most important coach in the game of life for your little girl is you.

We must help relieve the pressure on our children by offering magazine choices that teach them to take care of themselves instead of encouraging them to emulate near-naked super-models. We must let them know that their true beauty comes from within, from being confident, kind, and caring about other people. One excellent magazine designed to counter the cultural rot pushed on our girls is *Brio* (you can subscribe by going to FOTF.org). Engaging graphics, photos of girls of all shapes and sizes—who know how to dress fashionably instead of scantily—adorn the pages. My own daughter, Kristin, eagerly looks forward to receiving her monthly edition and is bolstered by the fun and entertaining articles that reflect a respect for her as a young woman rather than someone who should be *used*. And beyond magazines, today's moms must take a more active role in helping our daughters learn how to apply makeup, how to dress, and how to be truly feminine, without becoming obsessed with clothes, hair, and makeup.

Moms and Dads, we should be the ones molding and coaching our daughters through life, not some Madison Avenue advertising executive. Coaching your daughter means telling your ten-year-old how beautiful she is with just a clean face as you gently take the mascara wand out of her hand. (Can you tell I've done that before?) Coaching your daughter means unrolling the waistband on her shortened shorts and reminding her that she is a person of value. Coaching your daughter means taking the time, when passing the vulgar posters plastered on store windows in the mall, to say things like, "How sad that she feels she has to be next-to-naked in the mall to be important!"

THE BEST COACHES

Parents, just as a great sports coach sometimes yells, sometimes comforts, and always encourages, if you're to be a great character coach, you must too. The most successful coaches are not known by their toughness but rather by their commitment to challenging their charges to be better than the status quo. It's the same for you. And although coaching your son or daughter in life may sometimes take a lot of sweat and hard work from both you and your child, remember that the world's greatest coaches are marked both by the success of the athletes they train and their undying loyalty they feel for their coach.

Take Joe Gibbs, for example, one of the most successful coaches in the National Football League. Few NFL coaches have had a better winning percentage than Gibbs, who led the Washington Redskins to three Super Bowl victories. "And on those rare Sundays when the Redskins did lose, there were no public tantrums, not even once," *Washington Post* sports columnist Michael Wilbon once wrote. "Gibbs never blamed a player, never showed up an assistant by throwing a clipboard and going nuts on the sidelines. If something went wrong, he took the blame."

Gibbs's integrity, along with his all-too-rare combination of good sense, quick thinking, and hard work, did more than give Washington-area football fans something to cheer about. It inspired players to dig deep and play better, smarter, and harder than they might have under a less imaginative coach. Players such as running back Darrell Green enjoyed spectacular careers under Gibbs. And these players didn't contribute to their communities only on the playing field. Green founded the Darrell Green Youth Life Foundation in 1988 to help children who might otherwise fall through the cracks and fail to live up to their potential.

"Our children are our future, yet for too many children, the future is bleak," Green says. "In order to maximize the potential of our youth, it is necessary for caring adults to become actively involved in their lives." That attitude has led Green to open four Youth Life Learning Centers—in Washington D.C., Virginia, North Carolina, and Tennessee—to provide after-school programs that impart much-needed academic enrichment with a message of faith.

Why does Green do this? Partly because of his strong religious faith. But he also knows from experience the difference one caring adult can make in a child's life. Green's parents separated when he was ten, and he wound up moving with his mother and six siblings into a housing project. And who made a difference in his life at this critical juncture? According to Green, it was his high school track coach. From there, he went to college and to the NFL, where he would play for Gibbs. Today, instead of being a kid whose dreams died in a housing project, he's a famous former athlete and a man who helps kids avoid the failure that seemingly lurks around every corner.

Green's coaches, in other words, made a huge difference. It's the kind of difference you can make with your child if you're willing to take advantage of the once-in-a-lifetime opportunity of accepting the job.

You may not win a daily popularity contest with your child, but your efforts will most likely result in unexpected manifestations of their absolute love and respect for you.

I discovered a note typed into my Blackberry (the palm-sized electronic gizmo that keeps me organized) by Kristin when she was twelve. One day, while scrolling through a few notes, I came across a surprising title in the memo pad feature. It read, "To My Mommy."

I clicked on the heading, and up popped a poem my daughter had written and presented to me as a gift for Mother's Day the previous year. What made the Blackberry version so special was that it was the exact same poem and she was again presenting it to me as a special gift—even though we had been through a year of the "tweens" where I had taken very firm stands with her on her choices of music, clothing, and friends. She started out with an opening message that said, "Surprise!! I love you so much, and I always will!" She had then typed in the poem, which reads:

When I look into your eyes I see the colors of the setting skies,
I see the golden yellow sunlight of the perfect summer day,
Sparkling on the water of a crystal clear bay.
I see the glimmering stars above,
I see the spread wings of a peaceful dove,
I see the wonderful caring person that I so wish I could be,
And thank the Lord God Almighty,
That he chose you for me!
I love you! With love, from Kristin

13

THE DAILY BATTLE

You've read the facts, heard the admonishments, caught the vision.

So now what do you do?

To truly protect your children from a culture that's gone stark raving mad is to understand two intertwined principles that may sound contradictory at first: 1) Protecting your kids is a daily battle, and 2) You get one chance to do it right.

Parenting is not a dress rehearsal. You get one chance per child. So it's important to get it right the first time, because that's all there is.

But it is a daily battle. It takes a daily commitment to do those things you know are right. The good news is, every day is a new day. The chance to start over dawns with every new morning. When you make mistakes, when you fall to the pressure, you get to begin anew. The important thing to remember is that a day of not trying or giving up is a day that is lost forever. And, sadly, some mistakes can have a lasting impact.

Every single morning I awaken with a prayer in my heart and a resolve to stand true to the things in which I believe. I determine every day to uphold the values for my family that my husband

and I have chosen. I remind myself daily that when all is said and done, it is not my neighbor or my child's teachers or friends that will be held accountable for the choices I make for my children; it is my child that will either reap the benefits or suffer the consequences. And it is I who will someday stand before my Creator to give an account for what I did with and for the little lives that were entrusted to my hands.

When my children were very small, my husband and I visited Cherrydale Baptist Church in Arlington, Virginia, one Sunday morning, and I heard about the Jewish tradition of "blessing" children. It was both profoundly beautiful and powerful, and it is a lesson I have recalled many times throughout my motherhood.

The pastor of the church, Steve King, adapted this Jewish tradition into a wonderful ceremony for parents of young children. It's called "parent dedication."

Pastor King realizes that parents are going to be the single greatest influence on their kids' lives—whether for good or for bad. So he offers parents an opportunity to understand the essence of parenting and to publicly commit to doing it the right way.

He begins this most beautiful of services explaining the elements of what it means to bless children; the thoughts are from *The Blessing* by Gary Smalley and John Trent. The Old Testament patriarchs laid out a pattern that every parent should follow in raising children. The key elements for fully blessing a child on a daily basis are:

- Bless your child with loving, consistent, and meaningful touch

- Bless your children with spoken words that are positive and encouraging

- Bless your child by expressing that they have high value

- Bless your child by picturing for them a special future

- Bless your child with an active commitment to them as a person

This incredible, insightful understanding into God's vision for our children—and the love He would have us impart to them—is one reason we joined this church.

After having moved away for nine years, my husband and I have returned to this congregation with our teenagers and found that it is a thriving, growing, nurturing environment for families. We weren't surprised at all. We have rejoined the congregation and view our church as a partner in this, at times, overwhelming battle to impart kindness, gentleness, and self-control to our children.

As mentioned in Chapter Four, modeling faith in your own life is essential to your success in protecting your children. You must also find a body of people who share your values and will partner with you to reinforce them with your kids.

But there's something else that is key in your daily efforts to win the day and to secure the future for your precious little ones.

Mom or Dad may want to consider becoming a quitter.

That's right. If your family is made up of a mother with young children, who works outside the home for more than a few hours a day, and a father that also works, your family may just be better off—and I mean everyone in your family—if one of you leaves your job for a season.

My message is not politically correct, and my purpose is not to condemn those who must work. But I do want to challenge modern thought with a concept as basic to child-rearing as a healthy diet: quitting the rat race and the race to "keep up with the Joneses" is crucial to helping your children win as members of the human race. "I work because I have to" is the common initial response I get when I suggest that moms or dads be quitters. "We need the money!"

Perhaps it's time to define "need."

Do you really "need" an SUV, a bigger house, or a second or third television? Do your kids really "need" the latest Nintendo, name-brand clothes, or the fanciest scooter?

Moms, allow me to suggest something radical: what your children truly need is you.

And if you give kids a choice between a new car or more time with Mommy, Mom wins hands down.

Kids need dads too. However, with very young children, it's mothers who are—face it—equipped from the beginning to offer most of the care needed in the early months. Please don't be offended or think I'm sexist—I didn't give women milk-producing breasts and God didn't give them to men.

But that doesn't mean Dad can't quit for a time later on. The real point is to have at least one of you around in the formative years, and both of you around as much as possible.

Please don't fall into the materialistic trap at the expense of your own kids. A toddler doesn't know or care if she has two pairs of shoes or five. A young child doesn't understand the difference between a Navigator and a Neon. Do you think an eight-year-old even knows who Calvin Klein is? If she does, then you definitely need to quit.

It's time to ask yourself what you're really buying and why. Have you ever stopped to evaluate not just what you pay in dollars and cents for "things," but what you pay in time lost with your family?

Fathers and mothers must face the fact that the modern American family is in distress. With the pressures of dual careers, often no one is keeping the home fires burning. What families gain with an additional bread-earner, they often pay for with a loss of nurturing.

Gone are the leisurely family dinners and the important conversation that went with them. A study called "The Importance of Family Dinners" by the National Center on Addiction and Substance Abuse at Columbia University revealed that the more often teenagers have dinner with their parents, the less likely they are to smoke, drink, or use illegal drugs. "In fact," as The Heritage Foundation also reports, "compared with teens who have frequent family dinners, those who have dinner with their families only two nights per week or less are at *double* the risk of substance abuse." Family meals are also some of the best opportunities to build warm memories and actually have full sentence conversations with busy teens! If you aren't eating together as a family regularly, take the easy steps to plan simple meals ahead of time, divide up duties, and tweak your schedule so you can do so. Eating together provides you with some of the most enjoyable and most effective opportunities to show your kids just how much you love them.

Children often learn more from television, public influences, and transient adult relationships than they do from their own parents. Spending less time each day with their moms and dads and more time with an endless flow of randomly-assigned teachers and "care givers" has left children of all ages hungry for the richness and depth of fully developed mother/child and father/child relationships. Family members are like ships that pass in the night. They often get lost in the fog of life and crash on the reefs of loneliness and divorce. Everyone suffers, and children suffer most.

Women have made—and should continue to make—great contributions to the fields of business, science, and education. I'm not advocating that these roles be abandoned. I'm advocating that they be partially set aside for a season or engaged in for fewer hours a day. Women are particularly blessed with a life cycle that is composed of seasons. "To every thing there is a season, and a time to every purpose under the heaven" is a biblical truth from Ecclesiastes that obviously applies to women.

It has been said, "The hand that rocks the cradle rules the world," and, "A woman's place is in the house—and the Senate, and the White House." Both of these sayings are true, and they are *not* mutually exclusive. I've heard it expressed this way, "Women can have it all—we just can't have it all at once." How true.

When you experience the miracle and blessing of childbirth, when a hungry, helpless baby is placed in your arms, when this most precious and dependent of human beings is entrusted to your care, the season for mothering has clearly arrived.

Just as spring with all its beauty and promise is fleeting, so are the days of youth. Your children will be young only once, and oh, so briefly. Every hour away is an hour lost forever.

Don't buy the lie that "It's quality time, not quantity that counts." This is not an either/or situation. Children truly need and deserve both. Someone is going to be pouring habits, values, and emotions into your children. Let that someone be you.

Whatever financial sacrifices your family must make to enable you to raise your own children will be well worth the joy and memories for both you and your child—joy and memories that can't be bought.

Be creative in your quest for the extra income you want for life's little expenses. Sell something—Avon , Tupperware, whatever. Start a home-based business. If you're a professional, try to become a consultant. Find a part-time job. Today's technologies can be the great liberator of the family; talk to your boss about telecommuting for a while. More and more companies are beginning to understand that happier families make for happier employees. Do anything you can to get ahead—not in your career but in your role as mom and dad. Think outside the box. Fight the system to be with your kids.

Make it your life's mission to be the mommy or daddy your children were born for you to be.

A MAN IN THE MAKING

Perhaps one of my diary entries from 2002 best expresses what a tremendous blessing it is for us as parents when we begin to see the results of our efforts to fight the culture:

Deep, rich tones permeate the room and hang in the air like a dense, damp fog. *Boom, boom, boom.*

The vibrations from my son's bass guitar shake the walls of

my home office as they reverberate down the studs and through the framing. I stare intently at the family photograph that hangs across the room—it is rattling a bit with every beat. Even though Drew is upstairs in his bedroom, the notes are felt throughout our home as if they are living, pulsating creatures boldly oozing through the vents and paneling.

From my vantage point, it is impossible to distinguish one chord from another. *Boom, boom, boom*—the notes resonate again and again at varying intervals. The sounds created by my son's youthful touch are very much alive, yet surprisingly smooth.

I imagine what he must look like as his mind and spirit become one with the music. Drew is fifteen years old, and playing the bass and electric guitars has become his passion. Neither my husband nor I ever have to remind him to practice—to the contrary, there are many days and nights when we must gently point out his other responsibilities. At times he is so absorbed in his music that the vibrating *booms* seem to go on for hours. They have come to be among the sounds of life I most enjoy.

As this young lad of mine shuts his door and retreats into his magical musical world, I find great comfort and assurance in the man he is becoming. Drew's music folder is filled with scores of a style not normally found in a teenager's portfolio. Worship and praise music is what draws him to his creative place. This music somehow transforms our home into a tranquil oasis from the clutter and bustle of everyday life. I am amazed as I reflect on the fact that the introduction of even more sound and volume into our lives has the reverse effect of what would normally be expected.

Drew takes three guitar lessons a week and, on a fourth day, wakes on his own long before sunrise to prepare for an early morning chapel service at a local Christian high school of which he is not even a student. I marvel at his adherence to a commitment he has made to the church music director that requires him to exchange his warm bed for the opportunity to play with the chapel's praise team. It is Drew's choice each week to hold fast to this commitment or abandon it for a few hours of coveted sleep. Yet, week after week, he quietly dresses, fixes his own breakfast, and politely asks his father to drive him to the service.

It is in these moments—of practice, of service, of commitment—that I smile and think we must be doing something right. Parenting our three children is a pleasure that my husband and I relish. With every passing day it seems as though they are slipping faster and faster through our fingers, not unlike the proverbial sand through an hourglass. We have poured countless hours of love, teaching, patience, and education into them, all bathed in fervent prayers.

When unpleasant trials arise or bad attitudes crop up in our growing charges, I remind myself that they must be dealt with quickly and firmly. I am painfully aware that this act of parenting is not a dress rehearsal—I have but one chance per child to do it right. There is no giving in, no shrugging of the shoulders, no throwing up of the arms in hopelessness. It is my duty to hold fast, to stand firm, and to never, ever compromise the values and standards I would have my children claim as their own.

As Drew and his siblings begin to stretch their wings and venture further into the world, it intrigues me to watch them mature, develop, and experience independent life in small, measurable doses. And when they err, my husband and I are ready to quickly correct misjudgments and set them back on course. Until they are completely grown and leave for college, we view our home as a training ground provided by God to help establish within them the character and qualities that will enrich their lives and make our society and nation a better place.

Someday soon, the music Drew makes will not be within my hearing range. Until then, I treasure the beautiful sounds of a man in the making.

TOGETHER

The apple whizzed by her head so fast you could barely see it. Not to be outdone by her brother, Kristin grabbed a particularly putrid rotting apple from the ground and lobbed it at Drew with the greatest of delight. Ah, these are the moments family memories are made of!

It was a perfect crisp fall day accentuated by a cloudless sky of the clearest blue. We drove about ninety minutes from our home in D.C. to the beautiful Virginia countryside to pick apples. Along for the adventure were our "son" (okay, not really our son, but we love him like one), Michael; our two teen boys, Drew and Nick; and our then twelve-year-old daughter, Kristin. My husband and I had been planning the trip for several days, anticipating family time filled with the simple pleasures in life. We were not disappointed.

When you take three teenage boys and one younger sister on a road trip, you've got to make a conscious decision in advance that you *are* going to have a great time filled with the joys of teen-male antics—if you don't, you're likely to go nuts. It's also helpful if the little sister is a tough cookie. Our group has spent many hours of togetherness in the family van on such jaunts, and everyone sort of figured out their roles, mischievous tricks, defensive measures, and counter-attacks long ago. As my once-little children continue to grow older and taller and more occupied with their own activities and friends, I've come to relish such adventures.

How many more fall days are there for us to be together? It breaks my heart to realize that there's only what is left of this season and then just one more autumn for us to enjoy as a family. Drew is a junior in high school and will be headed off to college much too soon, only to be followed by Nick and Michael the next year. I'm learning the hard way—as so many parents before me have—that childhood is fleeting.

In today's incredibly busy, media-saturated world, I find it is ever more difficult to carve out time for our family to spend together. Even arranging family dinners can be a hassle—and sometimes you *get* hassled a bit by teens who think they're too mature for such togetherness. But coordinating schedules, turning off the tube, pushing other activities and homework aside, letting the dirty laundry sit, and ignoring all the other distractions of life that often rob us of the opportunity to be together are not only worth the effort, shutting out the world and concentrating on family is an essential element in producing healthy, happy kids.

The world has become a dangerous place for children. There's terrorism at home and war abroad to worry about. And so many negative influences attack their sensibilities every day that the only way they're going to *find* their way is if parents take the time to *show* them. Teaching kids values such as courage and integrity and how to rise above a sex-crazed culture that threatens their futures doesn't just come from having serious chats—it also comes from having wacky fun on a family road trip or from the simple act of eating together on a regular basis.

My colleagues at The Heritage Foundation have combed through massive amounts of social science research from peer-reviewed journals and found that kids whose parents spend time with them are less likely to smoke, abuse drugs, drink, or engage in sex. You can peruse the research yourself for free. Heritage researchers have also found that the best place for men, women, and children is in a loving home environment (this research, and more, is available at no charge on Heritage.org).

Our instincts tell us that individuals who live in loving families that spend time together make for better individuals—but how many of us actually *live* like we believe it? How many moms and dads have forgotten that what kids really want isn't another television, or more "stuff"; what they *really* want—and need—is time with *you*.

The trips don't have to be expensive or filled with endless planned activities and tours, and the meals don't have to be fancy. They just have to *be*. Whether it's taking the time for a walk in the park or a picnic, biking, or doing something a bit more conventional like providing the perfect environment for apple bomb wars, you'll be instilling in your children loving memories, values, and a sense of security. And, like anytime you give such blessings to others, you'll end up feeling pretty blessed yourself.

ONE DAY AT A TIME

Whenever I feel overwhelmed by the challenges of raising moral kids in an immoral, sexually charged world, I remind myself that all I have to do is take it one day at a time.

I have received tens of thousands of e-mails over the years from parents who read my weekly column, "Heart Beat," which discusses many of the issues covered in this book. The responses are usually so encouraging and helpful that I often read and re-read many of them when the going gets tough. Parents around the nation have reminded me we are comrades in a noble battle—and that we fight for nothing less than the hearts, minds, and souls of our children.

In order to encourage all of us in the beautiful, challenging, exhausting, and extremely rewarding role of parenthood, I'd like to share a little of the feedback with you. Many of the e-mails share practical tips and reminders for the daily battle.

- I once had a man write who blamed many of the cultural problems on ministers who won't point out evil from the pulpit. He's right. The preacher who fails in this task fails his congregation. I receive e-mail from many pastors around the country on a regular basis, and I know there are plenty of you who understand the importance of partnering with the parents in your congregation in an effort to raise children who love God, His truths, and His people. We're counting on you. Parents, if your church isn't supporting you in the battle, you may need to find a new congregation that does.

- A doctor from Louisiana pointed out what should be an obvious safeguard regarding electronic media that I've covered in this book but is overlooked in far too many homes and is worth repeating: don't let kids have computers or televisions in their own room. These devices are often windows to a seedy world. Parents need to make certain that harmful material does not invade our homes through those windows. In our home, our two computers are set up in a family office room, the door of which is always open, and our Internet access has a filter. And our televisions contain parental blocks to keep our kids from stumbling across garbage programming.

- Many parents have written to say the hard part isn't picking the right TV shows for children; it's avoiding offensive commercials. One said some of the worst ads come during the sporting events her husband watches. It's a good idea when watching television—even sporting events—with your kids, to keep the remote control handy, and to discuss with them why some commercials are inappropriate.

- One parent (with a great sense of humor) said to remember another handy tool, the microwave: "It does interesting things to bad CDs and DVDs that kids might otherwise fish out of the garbage." (Hmmm, I bet cooking CDs smells similar to dinner in the Hagelin house!)

- Another reader reminds us of the importance of having our children spend time with their grandparents and other extended family members. It provides them with a greater sense of security, a feeling of belonging. My own kids will never forget bicycling, enjoying family dinners or accompanying various aunts, uncles and cousins on trips. And although my parents are gone, my kids have memories of them they will always treasure. My husband's parents, our dear Mamma and Papa John, have provided my kids with plenty of warm memories and traditional values that will serve them for the rest of their lives. Recently my daughter was telling me of her "dream home." I was deeply touched when she said, "I want it to feel like Mamma John's house: warm, cozy, and handmade."

- Many have written to say they have recommitted to being the guardians of their homes. One called a column I wrote on the need to recommit to parenting our own children "a cold slap in the face." He vowed never to be lulled by the siren song of the crazy culture again.

- One stepdad wrote to say he had encountered the "fcuk" ads I described in *Teen People* magazine (see Chapter One). He explained to his stepdaughter why she couldn't read such trash in their home anymore. He said he wasn't punishing her, merely trying to protect her. He took a deep breath and then showed her the ad. "To my relief," he wrote, "she was just as incredulous and understood."

And that's the best part: the kids themselves. They want limits. They want borders. They want a clear sense of right and wrong. They're feeling around for those protective walls, for the steady, dependable standards they can count on in life.

Yes, they will learn about the world soon enough. But if, when that time comes, they're prepared to make proper moral judgments—the judgments you've helped them learn to make—then you've succeeded in the most important job in the world: parenting.

RESOURCES

It helps me to realize I'm not alone—and neither are you. Take heart. Plenty of folks out there care and want to help. Scores of resources are now available to make our jobs easier. I'm excited to provide you with a list of many from which my family has benefited. I've also included tips recommended via e-mail by readers of my "Heart Beat" column, which runs every week on WorldNetDaily.com and Townhall.com.

At Focus on the Family, for example, you'll find a lot of information to help parents, including offerings of teen magazines for boys and girls you can trust not to run ads like the one I've mentioned. The Internet can provide hours of entertainment, and the American Family Filter, a product of the American Family Association, can ensure that fun is safe. We use this tool on our home computers to protect our kids from venturing into sites that would harm them.

These are but a few of the tools you can employ now to protect your children. If you have favorites, share your recommendations with me, and I'll pass them on in a future column.

Stay connected, stay informed, and stick to your guns.

Remember, raising kids is not a dress rehearsal . . . you get one chance to do it right.

EDUCATION

ORGANIZATIONS

HomeSchoolInformation.com

> A great place to start looking for information on the ideals and many of the methods of "parent-directed education."

The Homeschool Legal Defense Association
(HSLDA.org)

> "A nonprofit advocacy organization established to defend and advance the constitutional right of parents to direct the education of their children and to protect family freedoms. Through annual memberships, HSLDA is tens of thousands of families united in service together, providing a strong voice when and where needed."

BOOKS

A Different Kind of Teacher: Solving the Crisis of American Schooling
> John Taylor Gatto
> Berkeley Hills Books

Books to Build On: A Grade-By-Grade Resource Guide for Parents and Teachers (**Core Knowledge Series**)
> E. D. Hirsch, John Holdren and the
> Core Knowledge Foundation
> Delta Trade Paperbacks

Cultural Literacy: What Every American Needs To Know
>   E.D. Hirsch Jr.
>   Vintage Books USA

Dumbing Down Our Kids: Why American Children Feel Good About Themselves But Can't Read, Write, or Add
>   Charles J. Sykes
>   St. Martin's Griffin

Dumbing Us Down: The Hidden Curriculum of Compulsory Schooling
>   John Taylor Gatto
>   New Society Publishers

Inside American Education
>   Thomas Sowell
>   Free Press

Let My Children Go
>   Ray Moore
>   Ambassador-Emerald International

The Book of Virtues
>   William J. Bennett
>   Simon & Schuster

The Children's Book of Virtues
>   William J. Bennett
>   Simon & Schuster

The Educated Child: A Parents' Guide from Preschool through Eighth Grade
> William J. Bennett, Chester E. Finn,
> and John T.E. Cribb
> Free Press

The Feel-Good Curriculum: The Dumbing Down of America's Kids in the Name of Self-Esteem
> Maureen Stout, Ph.D.
> Perseus Publishing

The Public Orphanage: How Public Schools Are Making Parents Irrelevant
> Eric Buehrer
> Thomas Nelson Publishers

The Schools We Need: And Why We Don't Have Them
> E. D. Hirsch
> Anchor Books/Doubleday

Why Johnny Can't Tell Right from Wrong and What We Can Do about It
> William Kilpatrick
> Simon & Schuster

Worldwide Guide to Homeschooling
> Dr. Brian Ray
> Broadman & Holman Publishers

ENTERTAINMENT

ORGANIZATIONS AND WEB SITES

AFAFilter.com

"Internet filtering software . . . reliable, accurate and FAST!"

ClearPlay.com

Perhaps the only thing preventing you from allowing your children to watch an otherwise-acceptable movie is one or two objectionable scenes—perhaps some bad language in a couple of places or a scene that's more violent that you feel it should be. If so, you may want to try "Clear Play," a service that lets you watch films without those elements. By ordering a special DVD player, you can flip a switch that allows you to skip over objectionable elements that you select ahead of time.

Media Research Center

325 S. Patrick Street

Alexandria, Virginia 22314

703-683-9733 or 800-672-1423

Fax: 703-683-9736

MediaResearch.org (or MRC.org)

Movieguide

A monthly magazine that helps parents gain a better understanding of the content of specific movies.

A one-year subscription is $40, but you can try it for free by going to Movieguide.org. (Reviews are also available on the Web site for new releases.) A typical Movieguide review rates the overall "moral acceptability" of the movie (from "exemplary" to "abhorrent") and covers what type of objectionable content (sex, language, violence) the film may have, along with—and this is crucial—the moral context in which these elements are deployed.

Parents Television Council
707 Wilshire Boulevard #2075
Los Angeles, California 90017
213-629-9255
ParentsTV.org
". . . bringing America's demand for positive, family-oriented television programming to the entertainment industry."

Plugged In
This monthly magazine is a Focus on the Family publication designed to help equip parents, youth leaders, ministers and teens with the essential tools that will enable them to understand, navigate and impact the culture in which they live.

PluggedInOnline.com
A Web site offering reviews of a wide variety of movies, music and television shows to help parents

make a more informed decision about what their children can see and hear. Plugged-In's movie reviews, for example, will offer a short summary of the story and then list the following: positive elements, spiritual content, sexual content, violent content, crude or profane language, drug and alcohol content, other negative elements and a conclusion.

ScreenIt.com

Another movie-review service available exclusively online. For $24.95 a year, parents can access very detailed reviews, including a full synopsis and list of folks in front of and behind the camera. They also tell you exactly what you'll see in terms of drug and alcohol use, blood and gore, disrespectful or bad attitudes, frightening scenes, guns and weapons, sex and nudity, violence and profanity. They even list "imitative behavior"—words and actions your impressionable children might want to try at home—and "topics to talk about."

The Christian Film & Television Commission

2510-G Las Posas Road, Suite 502

Camarillo, California 93010

770-825-0084

805-383-4089

MediaWiseFamily.com/organization.html

Books

Death by Entertainment
>Jeremiah Films

Glued to the Tube: The Threat of Television Addiction to Today's Family
>Cheryl Pawlowski
>Sourcebooks

Hollywood Vs. America
>Michael Medved
>Harper Collins/Zondervan Publishers

How We Got Here: The 70s: The Decade that Brought You Modern Life—For Better or Worse
>David Frum
>Basic Books

Kid Stuff: Marketing Sex and Violence to America's Children
>Diane Ravitch and Joseph P. Viteritti
>Johns Hopkins University Press

Mommy, I'm Scared: How TV and Movies Frighten Children and What We Can Do To Protect Them
>Joanne Cantor
>Harvest Books

See No Evil: A Guide To Protecting Our Children from Media Violence
> Madeline Levine
> Jossey-Bass

Shows about Nothing
> Thomas Hibbs
> Spence Publishing

Stop Teaching Our Kids To Kill: A Call To Action against TV, Movie and Video Game Violence
> Dave Grossman and Gloria Degaetano
> Crown Publishers

The Media-Wise Family
> Ted Baehr, Ph.D.
> Chariot Victor Publishing

The Other Parent: The Inside Story of the Media's Effect on Our Children
> James P. Steyer
> Atria Books

The Plug-In Drug: Television, Computers and Family Life
> Marie Winn
> Penguin Books

365 TV-Free Activities You Can Do With Your Child: Plus 50 All-New Bonus Activities
> Steven J. Bennett, Ruth Bennett, and Steve Bennett
> Adams Media Corporation

GENERAL RESOURCES ON FAMILY AND CULTURAL ISSUES

ORGANIZATIONS AND WEB SITES

American Decency Association
P.O. Box 202
Fremont, Michigan 49412
231-924-4050
Fax: 231-924-1966
AmericanDecency.org
> ADA's mission is "to educate its members and the general public on matters of decency; to initiate, promote, encourage and coordinate activity designed to safeguard and advance public morality consistent with biblical Christianity."

American Family Association
P.O. Box 2440
Tupelo, Mississippi 38803
662-844-5036
Fax: 662-842-7798
AFA.net
> AFA "represents and stands for traditional family

values, focusing primarily on the influence of television and other media—including pornography—on our society." AFA also operates the companion Web sites OneMillionDads.com, OneMillionMoms.com, and OneMillionYouth.com, all dedicated to stopping the exploitation of our children, especially by the entertainment media. Dad, OneMillionDads.com is the most powerful tool you have to stand against the immorality, violence, vulgarity and profanity the entertainment media is throwing at your children.

AskListenLearn.com and AskListenLearnParents.com

Nickelodeon and The Century Council have created a guide for kids that tells how to refuse alcohol and features interactive games.

Best Friends Foundation

4455 Connecticut Avenue, N.W., Suite 310
Washington D.C. 20008
202-237-8156
Fax: 202-237-2776
BestFriendsFoundation.org

The BFF "strives to provide a nationwide network of programs dedicated to the physical and emotional well-being of adolescents." Best Friends also sponsors the "Best Men" program, which is "designed to provide positive and healthy answers to the challenges facing boys today."

Boy Scouts of America, National Council
P.O. Box 152079
Irving, Texas 75015-2079
For information about Scouting in your area, please contact
your local council at
Scouting.org/nav/enter.jsp?s=xx&c=lc.

Center for the Study of Popular Culture
4401 Wilshire Drive, 4th Floor
Los Angeles, California 90010
323-556-2550
CSPC.org

Citizens for Community Values
11175 Reading Road, Suite 103
Cincinnati, Ohio 45241
513-733-5775
Fax: 513-733-5794
CCV.org

Concerned Mothers Alliance for Children (C-MAC)
233 Rogue River Hwy
Grants Pass, Oregon 97527
541-479-2322
C-MAC.org
> C-MAC provides a simple and effective system for
> churches to use against the corrupting influence of
> the pop culture. Clergy or lay leaders who think the
> women of their church might be willing to give one

hour every eight weeks to make a difference should register on this site for further information.

Concerned Women for America
1015 Fifteenth St., N.W., Suite 1100
Washington D.C. 20005
202-488-7000
Fax: 202-488-0806
CWFA.org

Crosswalk.com
"As a Christ-centered, for-profit corporation, we will create value for our customers, employees, and shareholders by:

- Bringing glory to God in all that we do;

- Equipping people to grow in their faith and the practical application of it in their lives;

- Enhancing fellowship, communication, and relationship-building within the Christian community; and

- Encouraging and enabling personal involvement in the care of those who are spiritually, emotionally, physically, or financially poor."

FamilyDatabase.org
"The Heritage Foundation's Family & Society Database catalogs social science findings on the fam-

ily gleaned from peer-reviewed journals, books, and government surveys. Serving legislators and staffers, journalists and writers, teachers and students, as well as clergymen and helping professionals, the Database makes social science research easily accessible to the non-specialist."

Family Research Council
801 G Street, N.W.
Washington D.C. 20001
202-393-2100
Fax: 202-393-2134
FRC.org

Focus on the Family
8605 Explorer Drive
Colorado Springs, Colorado 80920
719-531-3400 or 800-A-FAMILY (232-6459)
FOTF.org and Family.org

Institute for American Values
1841 Broadway, Suite 211
New York, New York 10023
212-246-3942
Fax: 212-541-6665
AmericanValues.org

OnePlace.com
> "The leading provider of Christian audio content on the Internet."

Probe Ministries
1900 Firman Drive, Suite 100
Richardson, Texas 75081
972-480-0240 or 800-899-PROBE
Probe.org
> "Renewing the mind, equipping the church, engaging the world."

The Heritage Foundation
214 Massachusetts Ave., N.E.
Washington D.C. 20002
202-546-4400
Fax: 202-546-8328
Heritage.org

Townhall.com
> "Townhall.com is a one-stop mall of ideas in which people congregate to exchange, discuss, and disseminate the latest news and information from the conservative movement. Townhall.com is committed to inform, educate, and empower the public through this emerging electronic medium."

Vision Forum Ministries
4719 Blanco Rd.
San Antonio, Texas 78212
1-800-440-0022
VisionForum.com

Wall Builders
P.O. Box 397
Aledo, Texas 76008-0397
817-441-6044
WallBuilders.com

> "An organization dedicated to the restoration of the constitutional, moral, and religious foundation on which America was built—a foundation which, in recent years, has been seriously attacked and undermined."

WorldNetDaily.com, Inc.

> "WorldNetDaily.com is an independent newssite created to capitalize on new media technology, to reinvigorate and revitalize the role of the free press as a guardian of liberty, an exponent of truth and justice, an uncompromising disseminator of news."

BOOKS

America's Godly Heritage
> David Barton
> WallBuilder Press

Beauty by the Book: Seeing Yourself as God Sees You
>   Nancy Stafford
>   Multnomah Publishers

Mind Siege: The Battle for Truth in the New Millennium
>   Tim LaHaye and David Noebel
>   Word Publishing

Taking America Back
>   Joseph Farah
>   WND Books

The Index of Leading Cultural Indicators
>   William J. Bennett
>   WaterBrook Press

The Things that Matter Most
>   Cal Thomas
>   Harper Collins/Zondervan

USA Today: The Stunning Incoherence of American Civilization
>   Reid Buckley
>   P.E.N. Press, Inc.

Who's Looking Out for You?
>   Bill O'Reilly
>   Broadway Books

LEGAL

ORGANIZATIONS

Alliance Defense Fund
15333 North Pima Road Suite 165
Scottsville, Arizona 85260
1-800-TELL-ADF
www.AllianceDefenseFund.org

American Center for Law and Justice
P.O. Box 64429
Virginia Beach, Virginia 23467
757-226-2489
Fax: 757-226-2836
ACLJ.org

> The American Center is a not-for-profit public interest law firm and educational organization dedicated to the promotion of pro-liberty, pro-life, and pro-family causes.

Pacific Justice Institute
P.O. Box 276600
Sacramento, California 95827
916-857-6900
Fax: 916-857-6902
PacificJustice.org

> The Institute is a nonprofit 501(c)(3) legal defense organization specializing in the defense of religious freedom, parental rights, and other civil liberties.

The National Law Center for Children and Families
3819 Plaza Drive
Fairfax, Virginia 22030-2512
703-691-4626
Fax: 703-691-4669
NationalLawCenter.org

> The National Law Center is a not-for-profit organization whose mission is the protection of children and families from the harmful effect of illegal pornography by assisting in law enforcement and law improvement.

The Rutherford Institute
P.O. Box 7482
Charlottesville, Virginia 22906-7482
434-978-3888
Fax: 434-978-1789
Rutherford.org

> An organization "dedicated to the defense of civil liberties and human rights."

Books

Bringing Justice to the People
       Edited by Lee Edwards
       Foreword by Edwin Meese III
       The Heritage Foundation

MARKETING

BOOKS

Branded: The Buying and Selling of Teenagers
    Alissa Quart
    Perseus Publishing

Consuming Kids: The Hostile Takeover of Childhood
    Susan Linn
    New Press

VIDEOS

Cultural Revival
    Bob Just
    "Discusses the core message of the PBS Frontline documentary, 'Merchants of Cool' and explains how corporations exploit your teens; how the pop culture functions and how it targets your children; how we can guide America's youth back to their God-centered identity; and why churches are key to the survival of America."

Send check or money order for $19 per video to:
    Bob Just Communications
    233 Rogue River Hwy
    Grants Pass, Oregon 97527

"Merchants of Cool"
60-minute documentary
2002, PBS Home Video
PBS.com

MARRIAGE

ORGANIZATIONS

Promise Keepers
P.O. Box 103001
Denver, Colorado 80250-3001
800-888-7595

> "Promise Keepers is dedicated to igniting and
> uniting men to be passionate followers of Jesus
> Christ through the effective communication of
> the 7 Promises."

The National Marriage Project at Rutgers University
54 Joyce Kilmer Ave., Lucy Stone Hall B217
Piscataway, New Jersey 08854
732-445-7922
Fax: 732-445-6110
Marriage.Rutgers.edu/

BOOKS

Back to the Family: Proven Advice on Building Stronger,
Healthier, Happier Family
   Raymond N. Guarendi
   Fireside Publishers

Getting Marriage Right: Realistic Counsel for Saving and Strengthening Relationships
> David P. Gushee
> Baker Books

Love for a Lifetime: Building a Marriage that Will Go the Distance
> James Dobson, Ph.D.
> Tyndale House Publishers

Putting Family First: Successful Strategies for Reclaiming Family Life in a Hurry-Up World
> William J. Doherty, Ph.D.,
> and Barbara Z. Carlson
> Owl Books

Soft Patriarchs, New Men: How Christianity Shapes Fathers and Husbands (Morality and Society Series)
> Brad Wilcox
> University of Chicago Press

The Proper Care and Feeding of Husbands
> Laura Schlessinger, Ph.D.
> HarperCollins Publishers

Ten Stupid Things Men Do To Mess Up Their Lives
> Laura Schlessinger, Ph.D.
> Quill Books

Ten Stupid Things Women Do To Mess Up Their Lives
Laura Schlessinger, Ph.D.
Harper Perennial Publishers

Woman Power: Transform Your Man, Your Marriage, Your Life
Laura Schlessinger, Ph.D.
HarperCollins Publishers

The Abolition of Marriage
Maggie Gallagher
Regnery Books

The Act of Marriage
Tim and Beverly LaHaye
Zondervan

The Broken Hearth: Reversing the Moral Collapse of the American Family
William J. Bennett
Broadway Books

The Case for Marriage: Why Married People Are Happier, Healthier, and Better Off Financially
Linda Waite
Broadway Books

The Marriage Problem: How Our Culture Has Weakened Families
> James Q. Wilson
>
> Perennial Currents

The Unexpected Legacy of Divorce: The 25-Year Landmark Study
> Judith S. Wallerstein, Julia Lewis, and Sandra Blakeslee
>
> Hyperion Publishers

What Wives Wish Their Husbands Knew about Women
> James Dobson, Ph.D.
>
> Tyndale House Publishers

Why Marriage Matters: Reasons To Believe in Marriage in a Postmodern Society
> Glenn T. Stanton
>
> Navpress Publishing Group

RESEARCH

From The Heritage Foundation (all of which can be accessed at Heritage.org):

- "Belonging to the Family and to God," a PowerPoint presentation by Patrick F. Fagan, March 29, 2004

- "The Positive Effects of Marriage: A Book of Charts" by Patrick F. Fagan, Robert E. Rector, Kirk A. Johnson, Ph.D., and America Peterson, 2004

- "The Social Scientific Data on the Impact of Marriage and Divorce on Children" by Patrick F. Fagan, May 13, 2004 (Congressional testimony)

- "Understanding the President's Healthy Marriage Initiative" by Robert E. Rector and Melissa G. Pardue, March 26, 2004 (Heritage Backgrounder #1741)

- "Marriage: Still the Safest Place for Women and Children" by Robert E. Rector, Patrick F. Fagan, and Kirk A. Johnson, Ph.D., March 9, 2004 (Backgrounder #1732)

- "The Effects of Divorce on America" by Patrick F. Fagan and Robert E. Rector, June 5, 2000 (Heritage Backgrounder #1373)

- "The Necessity of Marriage" by the Honorable Rick Santorum, October 20, 2003 (Heritage Lecture #804)

- "Increasing Marriage Would Dramatically Reduce Child Poverty" by Robert E. Rector, Kirk A. Johnson, Ph.D., Patrick F. Fagan, and Lauren R. Noyes, May 20, 2003 (Center for Data Analysis Report #03-06)

- "How Broken Families Rob Children of Their Chances for Future Prosperity" by Patrick F. Fagan, June 11, 1999 (Heritage Backgrounder #1283)

- "The Real Root Causes of Violent Crime: The Breakdown of Marriage, Family, and Community" by Patrick F. Fagan, March 17, 1995 (Heritage Backgrounder #1026)

- "Why Is It in the Government's Interest To Save Marriages?" by Michael J. McManus, February 25, 2002 (WebMemo #80)

- "Changing the Culture of Rejection," commentary piece by Patrick F. Fagan, May 20, 2004

- "The Return of the Ring," commentary piece by Melissa Pardue and Robert Rector, April 1, 2004

PARENTING

ORGANIZATIONS

Moms in Touch
P.O. Box 1120 Poway, California 92074-1120
1-800-949-MOMS
MomsInTouch.org

> Moms In Touch International is two or more moms who meet for one hour each week to pray for their children, their schools, their teachers, and administrators.

National Fatherhood Initiative
101 Lake Forest Boulevard, Suite 360
Gaithersburg, Maryland 20877
301-948-0599
Fax: 301-948-4325
Fatherhood.org

The Manners Club and Life Skills International
20530-24th Avenue, Suite 101
Langley, British Columbia, Canada V2Z 2A5
or in the U.S.:
10061 Riverside Drive, #200
North Hollywood, California 91602
604-530-4346
Fax: 604-530-2899

The Manners Club features Judi Vankevich, "The Manners Lady." She has produced a show-stopping, hand-clapping, rousing sing-along CD filled with songs to teach kids, from ages three to nine, good manners. Each song focuses on a different principle of character or manners. The three themes that are carried throughout the "Everybody Needs Good Manners" CD are the power of showing respect, living by the Golden Rule, and having an "attitude of gratitude."

Books

Bringing Up Boys: Practical Advice and Encouragement for Those Shaping the Next Generation of Men
James Dobson, Ph.D.
Tyndale House Publishers

Common Sense, No Frills, Plain English Guide To Being a Successful Dad
Ronald Klinger, Ph.D.
CSF Publishing

Everyday Graces
Karen Santorum
Intercollegiate Studies Institute

Father and Child Reunion: How To Bring the Dads We Need to the Children We Love
Warren Farrell, Ph.D.
Jeremy P. Tarcher

Fatherless America: Confronting Our Most Urgent Social Problem
David Blankenhorn
Harper Perennial Publishers

Life without Father: Compelling New Evidence that Fatherhood and Marriage Are Indispensable for the Good of Children and Society
> David Popenoe
> Harvard University Press

Motherhood & Hollywood
> Patricia Heaton
> Villard Books

Night Light for Parents: A Devotional
> James Dobson, Ph.D., Shirley Dobson
> Multnomah Publishers

Parenthood by Proxy: Don't Have Them If You Won't Raise Them
> Laura Schlessinger, Ph.D.
> HarperCollins Publishers

Parenting Isn't for Cowards
> James Dobson, Ph.D.
> W Publishing Group

Ready or Not: What Happens When We Treat Children as Small Adults
> Kay S. Hymowitz
> Encounter Books

*Saving Childhood: Protecting Our Children from the
National Assault on Innocence*
> Michael Medved and Diane Medved, Ph.D.
> Harper Perennial Publishers

*Stupid Things Parents Do To Mess Up Their Kids: Don't
Have Them If You Won't Raise Them*
> Laura Schlessinger, Ph.D.
> Quill Books

*Successful Fathers: The Subtle But Powerful Ways Fathers
Mold Their Children's Characters*
> James B. Stenson
> Scepter Publishers

Taking Sex Differences Seriously
> Steven E. Rhoads
> Encounter Books

*The Assault on Parenthood: How Our Culture Undermines
the Family*
> Dana Mack
> Encounter Books

The Complete Marriage and Family Home Reference Guide
> James Dobson, Ph.D.
> Tyndale House Publishers

The Disappearance of Childhood
>   Neil Postman
>   Vintage Books USA

The Epidemic: The Rot of American Culture, Absentee and Permissive Parenting, and the Resultant Plague of Joyless, Selfish Children
>   Robert Shaw, M.D.
>   HarperCollins Publishers

The Fatherhood Movement
>   Wade F. Horn, David Blankenhorn, and
>   Mitchell B. Pearlstein
>   Lexington Books

The New Dare To Discipline
>   James Dobson, Ph.D.
>   Tyndale House Publishers

The New Strong-Willed Child
>   James Dobson, Ph. D.
>   Living Books

The O'Reilly Factor for Kids: A Survival Guide for America's Families
>   Bill O'Reilly
>   Harper Entertainment

The Strong-Willed Child: Birth through Adolescence
    James Dobson, Ph.D.
    Tyndale House Publishers

The War against Boys
    Christina Hoff Sommers
    Simon & Schuster

RESEARCH

From The Heritage Foundation (all of which can be accessed at Heritage.org):

- "Teens Who Make Virginity Pledges Have Substantially Improved Life Outcomes" by Robert E. Rector, Kirk A. Johnson, Ph.D., and Jennifer A. Marshall, September 21, 2004 (Center for Data Analysis Report #04-07)

- "The Best Father's Day Gift," commentary piece by Patrick F. Fagan, June 13, 2002

- Family and Society Database

- "The Harmful Effects of Early Sexual Activity and Multiple Sexual Partners among Women: A Book of Charts" by Robert E. Rector, Kirk A. Johnson, Ph.D., Lauren R. Noyes, Shannan Martin, June 26, 2003

- "Sexually Active Teenagers Are More Likely To Be Depressed and To Attempt Suicide" by Robert E. Rector,

Kirk A. Johnson, Ph.D., and Lauren R. Noyes, June 3, 2003 (Center for Data Analysis Report #03-04)

- "Facts about Abstinence Education" by Robert E. Rector, March 30, 2004 (WebMemo #461)

PRAYER

ORGANIZATIONS

National Day of Prayer Task Force
P.O. Box 15616
Colorado Springs, Colorado 80935-5616
719-531-3379
Fax: 719-548-4520
A visit to the Task Force's Web site (NationalDayOfPrayer.org) will provide you with details of events and gatherings in your area.

The Capitol Hill Prayer Alert
1509 Shipsview Road
Annapolis, Maryland 21401
703-754-3629
PrayerAlert.org

BOOKS

A Different Kind of Strength: Rediscovering the Power of Being a Woman
Beverly LaHaye and Janice Shaw Crouse
Harvest House Publishers

Certain Peace in Uncertain Times: Embracing Prayer in an Anxious Age
> Shirley Dobson
>
> Multnomah Publishers

The Blessing
> Gary Smalley and John Trent
>
> Pocket Books

The Faith Factor in Fatherhood
> Don E. Eberly
>
> Lexington Books

The New Faithful: Why Young Adults Are Embracing Christian Orthodoxy
> Colleen Carroll
>
> Loyola Press

The Purpose-Driven Life: What on Earth Am I Here For?
> Rick Warren
>
> Zondervan

The Ten Commandments: The Significance of God's Laws in Everyday Life
> Laura Schlessinger, Ph.D.
>
> HarperCollins Publishers

Why You Can't Stay Silent: A Biblical Mandate To Shape Our Culture
>   Tom Minnery
>   Tyndale House Publishers

RESEARCH

From The Heritage Foundation (which can be accessed and downloaded free of charge on Heritage.org):

- "Religious Faith and Economic Growth: What Matters Most—Belief or Belonging?" by Robert Barro, Ph.D., and Joshua Mitchell, Ph.D., July 17, 2004 (Heritage Lecture #841)

- "Is Prayer Good for Your Health? A Critique of the Scientific Research" by Stuart M. Butler, Ph.D.; Harold G. Koenig, M.D.; Christina Puchalski, M.D.; Cynthia Cohen, Ph.D., J.D.; and Richard Sloan, Ph.D., December 22, 2003 (Heritage Lecture #816)

SEX

ORGANIZATIONS

Enough Is Enough
746 Walker Road, Suite 116
Great Falls, Virginia 22066
"Make the Internet Safer for Children and Families"
Sister site: ProtectKids.org ("Protecting kids in cyberspace")

Modest Apparel USA
66 Westfield Ave.
Ansonia, Connecticut 06401
866-269-0907
ModestApparelUSA.com

Modest By Design
801-256-0944
Toll Free: 1-866-715-6904
Fax: 801-562-8986
ModestByDesign.com
  "Clothing your father would approve of."

National Coalition for the Protection of Children & Families
800 Compton Rd., Ste 9224
Cincinnati, Ohio 45231
513-521-6227
Fax: 513-521-6337
NationalCoalition.org
  "Vision: To move the people of God to embrace, live out and defend the biblical truth of sexuality."

PamStenzel.com
  Pam Stenzel is an abstinence-education speaker who has addressed hundreds of thousands of teens nationwide. Her goal is to inspire young people to "embrace the benefits of character and abstinence

before marriage." She has a book and tape series called "Sex Has a Price Tag" that you can order from her Web site.

The Abstinence Clearinghouse
801 E 41st St.
Sioux Falls, South Dakota 57105
605-335-3643
Fax: 605-335-0629
Abstinence.net

The National Campaign To Prevent Teen Pregnancy
1776 Massachusetts Ave., N.W., Suite 200
Washington D.C. 20036
202-478-8500
Fax: 202-478-8588
TeenPregnancy.org

Web Wise Kids
P.O. Box 27203
Santa Ana, California 92799
866-WEB-WISE
WebWiseKids.com

> To "help ensure child Internet safety by giving tips and advice to parents and children on how to protect themselves from online predators."

BOOKS

Kinsey, Sex and Fraud: The Indoctrination of a People
Dr. Judith A. Reisman and Edward W. Eichel
Huntington House Publishers

Who Stole Feminism?
> Christina Hoff Sommers
> Simon & Schuster

RESEARCH

From The Heritage Foundation (all of which can be accessed at Heritage.org):

- "Comprehensive Sex Education vs. Authentic Abstinence: A Study of Competing Curricula" by Shannan Martin, Robert Rector, and Melissa G. Pardue, June 24, 2004

- "The Harmful Effects of Early Sexual Activity and Multiple Sexual Partners among Women: A Book of Charts" by Robert E. Rector, Kirk A. Johnson, Ph.D., Lauren R. Noyes, Shannan Martin, June 26, 2003

- "What Do Parents Want Taught in Sex Education Programs?" by Robert E. Rector, Melissa G. Pardue, and Shannan Martin, January 28, 2004 (Heritage Backgrounder #1722)

- "Government Spends $12 on Safe Sex and Contraceptives for Every $1 Spent on Abstinence" by Melissa G. Pardue,

Robert E. Rector, and Shannan Martin, January 14, 2004 (Heritage Backgrounder #1718)

- "The Effectiveness of Abstinence Education Programs in Reducing Sexual Activity among Youth" by Robert E. Rector, April 8, 2002 (Backgrounder #1533)

- "Good Money for Bad Advice" (January 15, 2004) and "When Sex Ed Becomes Porn 101" (August 27, 2003), both commentary pieces by Melissa Pardue and Robert Rector